Selections from the Restatement (Second) and Uniform Commercial Code for First-Year Contracts

2013 Statutory Supplement

Selections from the Restatement (Second) and Uniform Commercial Code for First-Year Contracts

2013 Statutory Supplement

Tracey E. George
Professor of Law and Professor of Political Science
Tarkington Chair in Teaching Excellence
Director, Cecil D. Branstetter Litigation & Dispute
Resolution Program
Vanderbilt University Law School

Russell Korobkin
Professor of Law
Faculty Director, Negotiation & Conflict Resolution Program
UCLA School of Law

Wolters Kluwer
Law & Business

Published by Wolters Kluwer Law & Business in New York.

Wolters Kluwer Law & Business serves customers worldwide with CCH, Aspen Publishers, and Kluwer Law International products. (www.wolterskluwerlb.com)

To contact Customer Service, e-mail customer.service@wolterskluwer.com, call 1-800-234-1660, fax 1-800-901-9075, or mail correspondence to:

Wolters Kluwer Law & Business
Attn: Order Department
PO Box 990
Frederick, MD 21705

Printed in the United States of America.

1 2 3 4 5 6 7 8 9 0

ISBN 978-1-4548-2793-1

SUSTAINABLE FORESTRY INITIATIVE
Certified Sourcing
www.sfiprogram.org
SFI-01234

SFI label applies to the text stock

About Wolters Kluwer Law & Business

Wolters Kluwer Law & Business is a leading global provider of intelligent information and digital solutions for legal and business professionals in key specialty areas, and respected educational resources for professors and law students. Wolters Kluwer Law & Business connects legal and business professionals as well as those in the education market with timely, specialized authoritative content and information-enabled solutions to support success through productivity, accuracy and mobility.

Serving customers worldwide, Wolters Kluwer Law & Business products include those under the Aspen Publishers, CCH, Kluwer Law International, Loislaw, ftwilliam.com and MediRegs family of products.

CCH products have been a trusted resource since 1913, and are highly regarded resources for legal, securities, antitrust and trade regulation, government contracting, banking, pension, payroll, employment and labor, and healthcare reimbursement and compliance professionals.

Aspen Publishers products provide essential information to attorneys, business professionals and law students. Written by preeminent authorities, the product line offers analytical and practical information in a range of specialty practice areas from securities law and intellectual property to mergers and acquisitions and pension/benefits. Aspen's trusted legal education resources provide professors and students with high-quality, up-to-date and effective resources for successful instruction and study in all areas of the law.

Kluwer Law International products provide the global business community with reliable international legal information in English. Legal practitioners, corporate counsel and business executives around the world rely on Kluwer Law journals, looseleafs, books, and electronic products for comprehensive information in many areas of international legal practice.

Loislaw is a comprehensive online legal research product providing legal content to law firm practitioners of various specializations. Loislaw provides attorneys with the ability to quickly and efficiently find the necessary legal information they need, when and where they need it, by facilitating access to primary law as well as state-specific law, records, forms and treatises.

ftwilliam.com offers employee benefits professionals the highest quality plan documents (retirement, welfare and non-qualified) and government forms (5500/PBGC, 1099 and IRS) software at highly competitive prices.

MediRegs products provide integrated health care compliance content and software solutions for professionals in healthcare, higher education and life sciences, including professionals in accounting, law and consulting.

Wolters Kluwer Law & Business, a division of Wolters Kluwer, is headquartered in New York. Wolters Kluwer is a market-leading global information services company focused on professionals.

Contents

Selections from the Restatement (Second) and Uniform Commercial Code for First-Year Contracts

2013 Statutory Supplement

EDITORS' INTRODUCTION

This book supplements contract law casebooks with carefully selected sections from two sources: the Restatement (Second) of Contracts and the Uniform Commercial Code (UCC). In the first-year Contracts course, these are the most important sources of law other than the judicial opinions that fill your casebook. The American Law Institute (ALI) drafts the Restatement, and along with the National Conference of Commissioners on Uniform State Laws (or the "Uniform Law Commission") authors the UCC, which is a model law.

THE RESTATEMENT (SECOND) OF CONTRACTS

The American Law Institute is a law-reform organization of American judges, lawyers, and law professors founded in 1923 "to address the uncertain and complex nature of early 20th-century American law."[1] ALI's founders believed "part of the law's uncertainty stemmed from the lack of agreement on fundamental principles of the common-law system, while the law's complexity was attributed to the numerous variations within different jurisdictions." To address these issues, ALI was "formed to improve the law and the administration of justice in a scholarly and scientific manner." ALI continues to serve that mission and currently has approximately 4,000 members selected through a nomination process.

The American Law Institute's first projects were "Restatements of Law" in nine core subjects, including contracts. A Restatement is intended to restate "basic legal subjects that would tell judges and lawyers what the law was" in order to "address uncertainty" in the common law. The process for producing each Restatement of Law follows common steps. A prominent legal expert in the subject area serves as the Restatement's "Reporter" and leads an advisory committee that drafts the Restatement of a specific subject. The committee examines common-law precedents and refines those judicial decisions into a simple statement of the law. The advisory committee submits the draft to ALI's membership for their review. The committee then revises the draft Restatement in response to the members' feedback. This submission-revision process is repeated numerous times over a span of multiple years. Once a consensus has been reached, a final version is submitted to the full ALI membership for approval. Restatements often reflect the approach of a majority of jurisdictions to a specific legal issue. But Reporters have proposed, and ALI members have adopted, modern or progressive positions on some issues, anticipating a shift in the common law and/or seeking to encourage such a change.

---

1. This quotation and others regarding ALI and its mission are taken from ALI's website: http://www.ali.org.

Restatements are addressed primarily to state courts, and their principles become law *only if* adopted and/or recognized in judicial opinions (or, less frequently, by legislatures). Absent such adoption, Restatements of Law are similar to other learned statements of the law such as treatises or scholarly articles. Yet Restatements typically have more wide-reaching influence than even the most important treatises. Parties may cite a Restatement section as persuasive authority to support the party's position, but the section is only binding on a court when adopted by a higher court within the jurisdiction as the controlling legal principle or doctrine on a question.

The Restatement of Contracts covers most of the essential principles of contract law. ALI has issued two editions of the Restatement of Contracts: the first in 1932, and the second in 1981. If a judicial opinion refers to the Restatement without an edition number, the court is referring to the First Restatement. Judges also may cite a draft version that had been circulated but not yet formally approved by ALI at the time of the court's decision. Since ALI took nine years to approve the first edition and nearly 20 to approve the second, draft versions circulated for many years.

The Restatement (Second) of Contracts includes 385 consecutively numbered sections, which are divided into 16 chapters. Each chapter focuses on a specific subject within contract law. The first chapter, for example, covers "Meaning of Terms." Each numbered section has a heading that states the rule covered by the section. The section names are important and should be used to inform your reading of the section and discernment of its purpose. Section 4, according to its heading, addresses "How a Promise May Be Made." The section states that "[a] promise may be stated in words either oral or written, or may be inferred wholly or partly from conduct." That is, a promise may be express or implied. In a judicial opinion, the court may cite this section by using the notation "Rest. (2d) Contracts § 4" or a similar abbreviation.

You will find *selected* sections of the Restatement (Second) of Contracts in this book. The more important a topic to the first-year Contracts course, the more extensive the coverage of that topic in this book. Thus, we include all sections on the meaning of core contract law terms, the formation of contracts, the doctrine of consideration, and the scope of contractual obligations. Most sections on defenses to enforcement and remedies also are excerpted. The book excludes sections beyond the scope of the great majority of first-year Contracts courses and/or that will (unnecessarily) confuse rather than inform your study. Sections focusing on contracts by seal, third-party beneficiaries, and delegation and assignment are excluded, for example.

In the unedited Restatement (Second) of Contracts, every section is followed by an explanatory "Comment," which includes "illustrations." We have been judicious in our inclusion of comments and illustrations, limiting the text to those likely to aid you in a first-year Contracts course. Thus, this supplement's version of § 4 includes "comment a" from the Restatement. The comment explains that the section is intended to make clear that the legal effect of a contract does not depend on the manner of formation. That is, a contract may be express or implied from surrounding circumstances.

THE UNIFORM COMMERCIAL CODE

Model laws, unlike Restatements of Law, are addressed to state legislatures, and occasionally the U.S. Congress, for enactment as statutes. ALI's most influential work may be its model commercial law—the Uniform Commercial Code (UCC)—which has been created in collaboration with the National Conference of Commissioners on Uniform State Laws. The Uniform Law Commission was created in 1892 to propose model legislation.[2] The organization is a non-partisan, non-profit organization of lawyers each of whom is selected by a state to serve as a uniform law commissioner.

The Uniform Commercial Code aims to be "a comprehensive code addressing most aspects of commercial law." The UCC covers ten subjects, each with its own numbered Article. The two articles most relevant to a first-year Contracts course are Articles 1 and 2. Article 1 provides definitions and explanations relevant to all of the subject-matter Articles. Article 1 does not create any independent substantive rights but instead operates in conjunction with other articles. Article 2 governs contracts for the sale of goods. Forty-nine states, the District of Columbia, and the U.S. Virgin Islands have adopted Articles 1 and 2 of the UCC.

This supplement includes selected sections and official comments from Articles 1 and 2 of the UCC. We have erred on the side of over-inclusion of the sections (or "black letter law") and under-inclusion of the official comments (which most state legislatures adopt as the relevant legislative history).

The Uniform Law Commission and ALI approved in 2001 a revised version of Article 1, which is included in this supplement. The significant changes include a clarification of the scope of Article 1, the inclusion of the "observance of reasonable commercial standards of fair dealing" as part of the definition of good faith, broader choice-of-law options for parties, and the addition of course of performance as a basis for contract interpretation. As of June 2013, 44 states and the U.S. Virgin Islands have enacted the revised version of Article 1.[3] Some enacting states have not adopted the

2. For the Uniform Law Commission's history and mission statement as well as updates on its current projects, visit its website: http://www.uniformlaws.org.

3. As of June 2013, Georgia, Missouri, New York, South Carolina, and Wyoming have not enacted and are not considering enacting the revisions. A bill has been introduced in Massachusetts, which has repeatedly failed to pass the revised version. Uniform Law Commission, Legislative Fact Sheet—UCC Article 1, General Provisions (2001), http://uniformlaws.org/LegislativeFactSheet.aspx?title=UCC Article 1, General Provisions (2001).

revision to the good faith definition, instead retaining the former definition, which defined good faith simply as "honesty in fact."

The Uniform Law Commission and ALI approved Article 2 revisions in 2003, but the 2003 revisions were withdrawn in 2011 because no state had enacted them. The only revision that has had some traction is an increase in the minimum price that triggers the requirement of a written contract for the sale of goods from $500 to $5,000 (the Statute of Frauds). We include the unrevised version (§ 2-201) but expect that jurisdictions are likely to increase the minimum price given the significant time that has passed since the $500 minimum was set.

CONCLUSION

The goal of this book is to provide the materials necessary to learn how to use the Restatement and a statute as part of the foundational course in Contracts. The book is not intended to be an independent source for either the Restatement (Second) of Contracts or the Uniform Commercial Code. It is instead a concise complement to your primary casebook.

Restatement (Second) of Contracts
Selected Sections

RESTATEMENT (SECOND) OF CONTRACTS
Selected Materials

The American Law Institute (Copyright 2012)

TABLE OF CONTENTS

TOPIC 3. MAKING OF OFFERS

TOPIC 4. DURATION OF THE OFFEREE'S POWER OF ACCEPTANCE

TOPIC 5. ACCEPTANCE OF OFFERS

CHAPTER 4. FORMATION OF CONTRACTS—CONSIDERATION

TOPIC 1. THE REQUIREMENT OF CONSIDERATION

TOPIC 6. SATISFACTION OF THE STATUTE BY A MEMORANDUM

§ 131. General Requisites of a Memorandum
§ 132. Several Writings
§ 133. Memorandum Not Made as Such
§ 134. Signature
§ 135. Who Must Sign
§ 136. Time of Memorandum
§ 137. Loss or Destruction of a Memorandum

TOPIC 7. CONSEQUENCES OF NON-COMPLIANCE

§ 138. Unenforceability
§ 139. Enforcement by Virtue of Action in Reliance
§ 143. Unenforceable Contract as Evidence
§ 144. Effect of Unenforceable Contract as to Third Parties
§ 145. Effect of Full Performance

CHAPTER 6. MISTAKE

§ 151. Mistake Defined
§ 152. When Mistake of Both Parties Makes a Contract Voidable
§ 153. When Mistake of One Party Makes a Contract Voidable
§ 154. When a Party Bears the Risk of a Mistake
§ 155. When Mistake of Both Parties as to Written Expression Justifies Reformation
§ 156. Mistake as to Contract Within the Statute of Frauds
§ 157. Effect of Fault of Party Seeking Relief

CHAPTER 7. MISREPRESENTATION, DURESS AND UNDUE INFLUENCE

TOPIC 1. MISREPRESENTATION

§ 159. Misrepresentation Defined
§ 160. When Action Is Equivalent to an Assertion (Concealment)
§ 161. When Non-Disclosure Is Equivalent to an Assertion
§ 162. When a Misrepresentation Is Fraudulent or Material
§ 163. When a Misrepresentation Prevents Formation of a Contract
§ 164. When a Misrepresentation Makes a Contract Voidable
§ 165. Cure by Change of Circumstances
§ 166. When a Misrepresentation as to a Writing Justifies Reformation
§ 167. When a Misrepresentation Is an Inducing Cause
§ 168. Reliance on Assertions of Opinion
§ 169. When Reliance on an Assertion of Opinion Is Not Justified

TOPIC 4. SCOPE AS AFFECTED BY USAGE

TOPIC 5. CONDITIONS AND SIMILAR EVENTS

CHAPTER 10. PERFORMANCE AND NON-PERFORMANCE

TOPIC 1. PERFORMANCES TO BE EXCHANGED UNDER AN EXCHANGE OF PROMISES

TOPIC 2. EFFECT OF PERFORMANCE AND NON-PERFORMANCE

§ 243. Effect of a Breach by Non-Performance as Giving Rise to a Claim for Damages for Total Breach
§ 249. When Payment Other Than By Legal Tender is Sufficient

TOPIC 3. EFFECT OF PROSPECTIVE NON-PERFORMANCE

§ 250. When a Statement or an Act Is a Repudiation
§ 251. When a Failure to Give Assurance May Be Treated as a Repudiation
§ 253. Effect of a Repudiation as a Breach and on Other Party's Duties

CHAPTER 11. IMPRACTICABILITY OF PERFORMANCE AND FRUSTRATION OF PURPOSE

§ 261. Discharge by Supervening Impracticability
§ 262. Death or Incapacity of Person Necessary for Performance
§ 263. Destruction, Deterioration or Failure to Come Into Existence of Thing Necessary for Performance
§ 264. Prevention by Governmental Regulation or Order
§ 265. Discharge by Supervening Frustration
§ 266. Existing Impracticability or Frustration
§ 271. Impracticability as Excuse for Non-Occurrence of a Condition

CHAPTER 12. DISCHARGE BY ASSENT OR ALTERATION

TOPIC 1. THE REQUIREMENT OF CONSIDERATION

§ 273. Requirement of Consideration or a Substitute
§ 279. Substituted Contract

TOPIC 2. SUBSTITUTED PERFORMANCE, SUBSTITUTED CONTRACT, ACCORD AND ACCOUNT STATED

§ 280. Novation
§ 281. Accord and Satisfaction

TOPIC 3. AGREEMENT OF RESCISSION, RELEASE AND CONTRACT NOT TO SUE

§ 283. Agreement of Rescission

CHAPTER 13. JOINT AND SEVERAL PROMISORS AND PROMISEES

[NOT EXCERPTED]

CHAPTER 14. CONTRACT BENEFICIARIES

[NOT EXCERPTED]

CHAPTER 15. ASSIGNMENT AND DELEGATION

[NOT EXCERPTED]

CHAPTER 16. REMEDIES

TOPIC 1. IN GENERAL

TOPIC 2. ENFORCEMENT BY AWARD OF DAMAGES

TOPIC 3. ENFORCEMENT BY SPECIFIC PERFORMANCE AND INJUNCTION

TOPIC 4. RESTITUTION

RESTATEMENT (SECOND) OF CONTRACTS
Selected Materials

FOREWORD

The Restatement of the Law of Contracts was approved and promulgated by the American Law Institute in May 1932, the first of the original Restatements to be finished. With Professor Samuel Williston as Chief Reporter and Professor Arthur L. Corbin as a Special Adviser and the Reporter on Remedies, the work was a legendary success, exercising enormous influence as an authoritative exposition of the subject.

It is implicit in the concept of restatement that the work should be kept current by periodic reexamination and revision. . . . Restatement, Second, of the Law of Contracts was begun in 1962 and completed by the Institute in 1979. During the intervening years, fourteen tentative drafts, the first of which appeared in 1964, were submitted for consideration. Contracts was thus on the agenda of the Annual Meetings in every year but two from 1964 through 1979. . . . The Reporters, their Advisers and the Institute approached the text of the first Restatement with the respect and tenderness that are appropriate in dealing with a classic. As the work proceeded, it uncovered relatively little need for major substantive revision, in the sense of changing the positions taken on important issues, although the Uniform Commercial Code inspired a number of significant additions. The opportunities presented for improving the black letter formulations involved primarily the mode of presentation: matters of organization, where changes in the ordering or scope of topics enhanced clarity or reduced redundancy, and matters of drafting, where revision served the interest of compression, simplification, precision or refinement of analysis.

INTRODUCTORY NOTE: A persistent source of difficulty in the law of contracts is the fact that words often have different meanings to the speaker and to the hearer. Most words are commonly used in more than one sense, and the words used in this Restatement are no exception. It is arguable that the difficulty is increased rather than diminished by an attempt to give a word a single definition and to use it only as defined. But where usage varies widely, definition makes it possible to avoid circumlocution in the statement of rules and to hold ambiguity to a minimum.

In the Restatement, an effort has been made to use only words with connotations familiar to the legal profession, and not to use two or more words to express the same legal concept. Where a word frequently used has a variety of distinct meanings, one meaning has been selected and indicated by definition. But it is obviously impossible to capture in a definition an entire complex institution such as "contract" or "promise." The operative facts necessary or sufficient to create legal relations and the legal relations created by those facts will appear with greater fullness in the succeeding chapters.

CHAPTER 1 MEANING OF TERMS

§1. Contract Defined

A contract is a promise or a set of promises for the breach of which the law gives a remedy, or the performance of which the law in some way recognizes as a duty.

§2. Promise; Promisor; Promisee; Beneficiary

(1) A promise is a manifestation of intention to act or refrain from acting in a specified way, so made as to justify a promisee in understanding that a commitment has been made.

(2) The person manifesting the intention is the promisor.

(3) The person to whom the manifestation is addressed is the promisee.

(4) Where performance will benefit a person other than the promisee, that person is a beneficiary.

Comment:

d. Promise of event beyond human control; warranty. Words which in terms promise that an event not within human control will occur may be interpreted to include a promise to answer for harm caused by the failure of the event to occur. An example is a warranty of an existing or past fact, such as a warranty that a horse is sound, or that a ship arrived in a foreign port some days previously. Such promises are often made when the parties are ignorant of the actual facts regarding which they bargain, and may be dealt with as if the warrantor could cause the fact to be as he asserted. It is then immaterial that the actual condition of affairs may be irrevocably fixed before the promise is made.

Words of warranty, like other conduct, must be interpreted in the light of the circumstances and the reasonable expectations of the parties. In an insurance contract, a "warranty" by the insured is usually not a promise at all; it may be merely a representation of fact, or, more commonly, the fact warranted is a condition of the insurer's duty to pay (see § 225(3)). In the sale of goods, on the other hand, a similar warranty normally also includes a promise to answer for damages (see Uniform Commercial Code § 2-715).

Illustration:

1. A, the builder of a house, or the inventor of the material used in part of its construction, says to B, the owner of the house, "I warrant that this house will never burn down." This includes a promise to pay for harm if the house should burn down.

f. Opinions and predictions. A promise must be distinguished from a statement of opinion or a mere prediction of future events. The distinction is not usually difficult in the case of an informal gratuitous opinion, since there is often no manifestation of intention to act or refrain from acting or to bring about a result, no expectation of performance and no consideration. The problem is frequently presented, however, whether words of a seller of goods amount to a warranty. Under Uniform Commercial Code § 2-313(2) a statement purporting to be merely the seller's opinion does not create a warranty, but the buyer's reliance on the seller's skill and judgment may create an implied warranty that the goods are fit for a particular purpose under Uniform Commercial Code § 2-315. In any case where an expert opinion is paid for, there is likely to be an implied promise that the expert will act with reasonable care and skill.

A promise often refers to future events which are predicted or assumed rather than promised. Thus a promise to render personal service at a particular future time commonly rests on an assumption that the promisor will be alive and well at that time; a promise to paint a building may similarly rest on an assumption that the building will be in existence. Such cases are the subject of Chapter 11. The promisor may of course promise to answer for harm caused by the failure of the future event to occur; if he does not, such a failure may discharge any duty of performance.

Illustration:

4. A, on seeing a house of thoroughly fireproof construction, says to B, the owner, "This house will never burn down." This is not a promise but merely an opinion or prediction. If A had been paid for his opinion as an expert, there might be an implied promise that he would employ reasonable care and skill in forming and giving his opinion.

§ 3. Agreement Defined; Bargain Defined

An agreement is a manifestation of mutual assent on the part of two or more persons. A bargain is an agreement to exchange promises or to exchange a promise for a performance or to exchange performances.

§ 4. How a Promise May Be Made

A promise may be stated in words either oral or written, or may be inferred wholly or partly from conduct.

Comment:

a. Express and implied contracts. Contracts are often spoken of as express or implied. The distinction involves, however, no difference in legal effect, but lies merely in the mode of manifesting assent. Just as assent may be manifested by words or other conduct, sometimes including silence, so intention to make a promise may be manifested in language or by implication from other circumstances, including course of dealing or usage of trade or course of performance. See Uniform Commercial Code § 1-201(3), defining "agreement."

Illustrations:

1. A telephones to his grocer, "Send me a ten-pound bag of flour." The grocer sends it. A has thereby promised to pay the grocer's current price therefor.

2. A, on passing a market where he has an account, sees a box of apples marked "25 cts. each." A picks up an apple, holds it up so the clerk in the establishment sees the act. The clerk nods, and A passes on. A has promised to pay twenty-five cents for the apple.

b. Quasi-contracts. Implied contracts are different from quasi-contracts, although in some cases the line between the two is indistinct. See Comment *a* to § 19. Quasi-contracts have often been called implied contracts or contracts implied in law; but, unlike true contracts, quasi-contracts are not based on the apparent intention of the parties to undertake the performances in question, nor are they promises. They are obligations created by law for reasons of justice. Such obligations were ordinarily enforced at common law in the same form of action (assumpsit) that was appropriate to true contracts, and some confusions with reference to the nature of quasi-contracts has been caused thereby. They are dealt with in the Restatement of Restitution. . . .

§ 5. Terms of Promise, Agreement, or Contract

(1) A term of a promise or agreement is that portion of the intention or assent manifested which relates to a particular matter.

(2) A term of a contract is that portion of the legal relations resulting from the promise or set of promises which relates to a particular matter, whether or not the parties manifest an intention to create those relations.

§ 6. Formal Contracts

The following types of contracts are subject in some respects to special rules that depend on their formal characteristics and differ from those governing contracts in general:

(a) Contracts under seal,

(b) Recognizances,

(c) Negotiable instruments and documents,

(d) Letters of credit.

§ 7. Voidable Contracts

A voidable contract is one where one or more parties have the power, by a manifestation of election to do so, to avoid the legal relations created by the contract, or by ratification of the contract to extinguish the power of avoidance.

Comment:

a. "Void contracts." A promise for breach of which the law neither gives a remedy nor otherwise recognizes a duty of performance by the promisor is often called a void contract. Under § 1, however, such a promise is not a contract at all; it is the "promise" or "agreement" that is void of legal effect. If the term "contract" were defined to refer to the acts of the parties without regard to their legal effect, a contract could without inconsistency be referred to as "void."

b. Grounds of avoidance. Typical instances of voidable contracts are those where one party was an infant, or where the contract was induced by fraud, mistakes, or duress, or where breach of a warranty or other promise justifies the aggrieved party in putting an end to the contract. Usually the power to avoid is confined to one party to the contract, but where, for instance, both parties are infants, or where both parties enter into a contract under a mutual mistake, the contract may be voidable by either one of the parties. Avoidance is often referred to as "disaffirmance."

§ 8. Unenforceable Contracts

An unenforceable contract is one for the breach of which neither the remedy of damages nor the remedy of specific performance is available, but which is recognized in some other way as creating a duty of performance, though there has been no ratification.

Comment:

a. Distinction between "voidable" and "unenforceable." Just as a contract may be voidable by one party or by either party, so it may be enforceable by one and not by the other or it may be unenforceable by either. Similarly, one party to an unenforceable contract may have a power to make the contract enforceable by all the usual remedies and both voidable and unenforceable contracts may have collateral consequences. Voidable contracts might be defined as one type of unenforceable contract. . . .

CHAPTER 2 FORMATION OF CONTRACTS—PARTIES AND CAPACITY

§ 9. Parties Required

There must be at least two parties to a contract, a promisor and a promisee, but there may be any greater number.

§10. Multiple Promisors and Promisees of the Same Performance

(1) Where there are more promisors than one in a contract, some or all of them may promise the same performance, whether or not there are also promises of separate performances.

(2) Where there are more promisees than one in a contract, a promise may be made to some or all of them as a unit, whether or not the same or another performance is separately promised to one or more of them.

§11. When a Person May Be Both Promisor and Promisee

A contract may be formed between two or more persons acting as a unit and one or more but fewer than all of these persons, acting either singly or with other persons.

§12. Capacity to Contract

(1) No one can be bound by contract who has not legal capacity to incur at least voidable contractual duties. Capacity to contract may be partial and its existence in respect of a particular transaction may depend upon the nature of the transaction or upon other circumstances.

(2) A natural person who manifests assent to a transaction has full legal capacity to incur contractual duties thereby unless he is

(a) under guardianship, or
(b) an infant, or
(c) mentally ill or defective, or
(d) intoxicated.

§13. Persons Affected by Guardianship

A person has no capacity to incur contractual duties if his property is under guardianship by reason of an adjudication of mental illness or defect.

§14. Infants

Unless a statute provides otherwise, a natural person has the capacity to incur only voidable contractual duties until the beginning of the day before the person's eighteenth birthday.

Comment:

c. Restoration of consideration. An infant need not take any action to disaffirm his contracts until he comes of age. If sued upon the contract, he may defend on the ground of infancy without returning the consideration received. His disaffirmance revests in the other party the title to any property received by the infant under the contract. If the consideration received by the infant has been dissipated by him, the other party is without remedy unless the infant ratifies the contract after coming of age or is under some non-contractual obligation. But some states, by statute or decision, have restricted the power of disaffirmance, either generally or under particular circumstances, by requiring restoration of the consideration received. Where the infant seeks to enforce the contract, the conditions of the other party's promise must be fulfilled. The problems arising when an infant seeks to disaffirm a conveyance or executed contract are beyond the scope of the Restatement of this Subject, whether the disaffirmance is attempted before or after he comes of age. As to what constitutes ratification, see § 85.

§ 15. Mental Illness or Defect

(1) A person incurs only voidable contractual duties by entering into a transaction if by reason of mental illness or defect

(a) he is unable to understand in a reasonable manner the nature and consequences of the transaction, or

(b) he is unable to act in a reasonable manner in relation to the transaction and the other party has reason to know of his condition.

(2) Where the contract is made on fair terms and the other party is without knowledge of the mental illness or defect, the power of avoidance under Subsection (1) terminates to the extent that the contract has been so performed in whole or in part or the circumstances have so changed that avoidance would be unjust. In such a case a court may grant relief as justice requires.

Comment:

a. Rationale. A contract made by a person who is mentally incompetent requires the reconciliation of two conflicting policies: the protection of justifiable expectations and of the security of transactions, and the protection of persons unable to protect themselves against imposition. Each policy has sometimes prevailed to a greater extent than is stated in this Section. At one extreme, it has been said that a lunatic has no capacity to contract because he has no mind; this view has given way to a better understanding of mental phenomena and to the doctrine that contractual obligation depends on manifestation of assent rather than on mental assent. See §§ 2, 19. At the other extreme, it has been asserted that mental incompetency has no effect on a contract unless other grounds of avoidance are present, such as fraud, undue influence, or gross inadequacy of consideration; it is now widely believed that such a rule gives inadequate protection to the incompetent and his family, particularly where the contract is entirely executory.

b. The standard of competency. It is now recognized that there is a wide variety of types and degrees of mental incompetency. Among them are congenital deficiencies in intelligence, the mental deterioration of old age, the effects of brain damage caused by accident or organic disease, and mental illnesses evidenced by such symptoms as delusions, hallucinations, delirium, confusion and depression. Where no guardian has been appointed, there is full contractual capacity in any case unless the mental illness or defect has affected the particular transaction: a person may be able to understand almost nothing, or only simple or routine transactions, or he may be incompetent only with respect to a particular type of transaction. Even though understanding is complete, he may lack the ability to control his acts in the way that the normal individual can and does control them; in such cases the inability makes the contract voidable only if the other party has reason to know of his condition. Where a person has some understanding of a particular transaction which is affected by mental illness or defect, the controlling consideration is whether the transaction in its result is one which a reasonably competent person might have made.

c. Proof of incompetency. Where there has been no previous adjudication of incompetency, the burden of proof is on the party asserting incompetency. Proof of irrational or unintelligent behavior is essential; almost any conduct of the person may be relevant, as may lay and expert opinions and prior and subsequent adjudications of incompetency. Age, bodily infirmity or disease, use of alcohol or drugs, and illiteracy may bolster other evidence of incompetency. Other facts have significance when there is mental illness or defect but some understanding: absence of independent advice, confidential or fiduciary relationship, undue influence, fraud, or secrecy; in such cases the critical fact often is departure from the normal pattern of similar transactions, and particularly inadequacy of consideration.

d. Operative effect of incompetency. Where no guardian has been appointed, the effect on executory contracts of incompetency by reason of mental illness or defect is very much like that of infancy. Regardless of the other party's knowledge or good faith and regardless of the fairness of the terms, the incompetent person on regaining full capacity may affirm or disaffirm the contract, or the power to affirm or disaffirm may be exercised on his behalf by his guardian or after his death by his personal representative. There may, however, be related obligations imposed by law independently of contract which cannot be disaffirmed. . . . And if the other party did not know of the incompetency at the time of contracting he cannot be compelled to perform unless the contract is effectively affirmed.

Illustration:

2. A, an incompetent not under guardianship, contracts to sell land to B, who does not know of the incompetency. A continues to be incompetent. On discovering the incompetency, B may refuse to perform until a guardian is

appointed, and if none is appointed within a reasonable time may obtain a decree cancelling the contract.

e. Effect of performance. Where the contract has been performed in whole or in part, avoidance is permitted only on equitable terms. In the traditional action at law, the doing of equity by or on behalf of the incompetent was accomplished by a tender before suit, but in equity or under modern merged procedure it is provided for in the decree. Any benefits still retained by the incompetent must be restored or paid for, and restitution must be made for any necessaries furnished under the contract. . . . If the other party knew of the incompetency at the time of contracting, or if he took unfair advantage of the incompetent, consideration not received by the incompetent or dissipated without benefit to him need not be restored.

Illustration:

3. A, an incompetent not under guardianship, contracts to buy land for a fair price from B, who does not know of the incompetency. Shortly after transfer of title to A and part payment by A, A dies. A's personal representative may recover A's part payment on reconveying the land to B.

f. When avoidance is inequitable. If the contract is made on fair terms and the other party has no reason to know of the incompetency, performance in whole or in part may so change the situation that the parties cannot be restored to their previous positions or may otherwise render avoidance inequitable. The contract then ceases to be voidable. Where the other party, though acting in good faith, had reason to know of the incompetency at the time of contracting or performance, or where the equities can be partially adjusted by the decree, the court may grant or deny relief as the situation requires. Factors to be taken into account in such cases include not only benefits conferred and received on both sides but also the extent to which avoidance will benefit the incompetent and the extent to which others who will benefit from avoidance had opportunities to prevent the situation from arising.

§ 16. Intoxicated Persons

A person incurs only voidable contractual duties by entering into a transaction if the other party has reason to know that by reason of intoxication

(a) he is unable to understand in a reasonable manner the nature and consequences of the transaction, or

(b) he is unable to act in a reasonable manner in relation to the transaction.

Comment:

b. What contracts are voidable. The standard of competency in intoxication cases is the same as that in cases of mental illness. If the intoxication is so extreme as to prevent any manifestation of assent, there is no contract. Otherwise the other party is affected only by intoxication of which he has reason to know. A contract made by a person who is so drunk he does not know what he is doing is voidable if the other party has reason to know of the intoxication. Where there is some understanding of the transaction despite intoxication, avoidance depends on a showing that the other party induced the drunkenness or that the consideration was inadequate or that the transaction departed from the normal pattern of similar transactions; if the particular transaction in its result is one which a reasonably competent person might have made, it cannot be avoided even though entirely executory.

Illustration:

1. A, while in a state of extreme intoxication, signs and mails a written offer on fair terms to B, who has no reason to know of the intoxication. B accepts the offer. A has no right to avoid the contract.

c. *Ratification and avoidance*. Where a contract is voidable on the ground of intoxication, the rules as to ratification and avoidance are much the same as in cases of misrepresentation. See Chapter 7. On becoming sober, the intoxicated person must act promptly to disaffirm and must offer to restore consideration received. Such an offer may be excused, however, if the consideration has been dissipated during the period of drunkenness.

Illustration:

4. A buys a barber shop from B for $650. Shortly afterward, A, helplessly drunk and evidently not aware of what he is doing, sells the shop back to B for $200. On recovering his senses, A cannot remember the transaction and cannot find out what happened to the $200. On prompt disaffirmance, A may recover the shop without repaying the $200.

CHAPTER 3 FORMATION OF CONTRACTS—MUTUAL ASSENT

TOPIC 1. IN GENERAL

§ 17. Requirement of a Bargain

(1) Except as stated in Subsection (2), the formation of a contract requires a bargain in which there is a manifestation of mutual assent to the exchange and a consideration.

(2) Whether or not there is a bargain a contract may be formed under special rules applicable to formal contracts or under the rules stated in §§ 82-94.

Comment:

c. *"Meeting of the minds."* The element of agreement is sometimes referred to as a "meeting of the minds." The parties to most contracts give actual as well as apparent assent, but it is clear that a mental reservation of a party to a bargain does not impair the obligation he purports to undertake. The phrase used here, therefore, is "manifestation of mutual assent," as in the definition of "agreement" in § 3.

d. "Sufficient consideration." The element of exchange is embodied in the concept of consideration. In some cases a promise is not binding for want of consideration, despite the presence of an element of exchange. "Consideration" has sometimes been used to refer to the element of exchange, without regard to whether it is sufficient to make an informal promise legally binding; the consideration which satisfies the legal requirement has then been called "sufficient consideration." As the term "consideration" is used here, however, it refers to an element of exchange which is legally sufficient, and the word "sufficient" would therefore be redundant.

TOPIC 2. MANIFESTATION OF ASSENT IN GENERAL

§ 18. Manifestation of Mutual Assent

Manifestation of mutual assent to an exchange requires that each party either make a promise or begin or render a performance.

§ 19. Conduct as Manifestation of Assent

(1) The manifestation of assent may be made wholly or partly by written or spoken words or by other acts or by failure to act.

(2) The conduct of a party is not effective as a manifestation of his assent unless he intends to engage in the conduct and knows or has reason to know that the other party may infer from his conduct that he assents.

(3) The conduct of a party may manifest assent even though he does not in fact assent. In such cases a resulting contract may be voidable because of fraud, duress, mistake, or other invalidating cause.

Comment:

a. Conduct other than words. Words are not the only medium of expression. Conduct may often convey as clearly as words a promise or an assent to a proposed promise.

Like words, non-verbal conduct often has different meanings to different people. Indeed, the meaning of conduct not used as a conventional symbol is more uncertain and more dependent on its setting than are words. A wide variety of elements of the total situation may be relevant to the interpretation of such conduct.

b. "Reason to know." A person has reason to know a fact, present or future, if he has information from which a person of ordinary intelligence would infer that the fact in question does or will exist. A person of superior intelligence has reason to know a fact if he has information from which a person of his intelligence would draw the inference. There is also reason to know if the inference would be that there is such a substantial chance of the existence of the fact that, if exercising reasonable care with reference to the matter in question, the person would predicate his action upon the assumption of its possible existence.

Reason to know is to be distinguished from knowledge and from "should know." Knowledge means conscious belief in the truth of a fact; reason to know need not be conscious. "Should know" imports a duty to others to ascertain facts; the words "reason to know" are used both where the actor has a duty to another and where he would not be acting adequately in the protection of his own interests were he not acting with reference to the facts which he has reason to know.

c. Responsibility for unintended appearance of assent. A "manifestation" of assent is not a mere appearance; the party must in some way be responsible for the appearance. There must be conduct and a conscious will to engage in that conduct.

§ 20. Effect of Misunderstanding

(1) There is no manifestation of mutual assent to an exchange if the parties attach materially different meanings to their manifestations and

(a) neither party knows or has reason to know the meaning attached by the other; or

(b) each party knows or each party has reason to know the meaning attached by the other.

(2) The manifestations of the parties are operative in accordance with the meaning attached to them by one of the parties if

(a) that party does not know of any different meaning attached by the other, and the other knows the meaning attached by the first party; or

(b) that party has no reason to know of any different meaning attached by the other, and the other has reason to know the meaning attached by the first party.

Comment:

b. The need for interpretation. The meaning given to words or other conduct depends to a varying extent on the context and on the prior experience of the parties. Almost never are all the connotations of a bargain exactly identical for both parties; it is enough that there is a core of common meaning sufficient to determine their performances with reasonable certainty or to give a reasonably certain basis for an appropriate legal remedy. See § 33. But material differences of meaning are a standard cause of contract disputes, and the decision of such disputes necessarily requires interpretation of the language and other conduct of the parties in light of the circumstances.

§ 21. Intention to Be Legally Bound

Neither real nor apparent intention that a promise be legally binding is essential to the formation of a contract, but a manifestation of intention that a promise shall not affect legal relations may prevent the formation of a contract.

§ 22. Mode of Assent: Offer and Acceptance

(1) The manifestation of mutual assent to an exchange ordinarily takes the form of an offer or proposal by one party followed by an acceptance by the other party or parties.

(2) A manifestation of mutual assent may be made even though neither offer nor acceptance can be identified and even though the moment of formation cannot be determined.

§ 23. Necessity That Manifestations Have Reference to Each Other

It is essential to a bargain that each party manifest assent with reference to the manifestation of the other.

TOPIC 3. MAKING OF OFFERS

§ 24. Offer Defined

An offer is the manifestation of willingness to enter into a bargain, so made as to justify another person in understanding that his assent to that bargain is invited and will conclude it.

§ 25. Option Contracts

An option contract is a promise which meets the requirements for the formation of a contract and limits the promisor's power to revoke an offer.

Comment:

a. "Option." A promise which constitutes an option contract may be contained in the offer itself, or it may be made separately in a collateral offer to keep the main offer open. Such promises are commonly called "options." But the word "option" is also often used for any continuing offer, even though revocable, and indeed is sometimes used to refer to any power to make a choice. To avoid ambiguity the phrase "option contract" is used in this Restatement.

b. The need for irrevocable offers. To provide the offeree with a dependable basis for decision whether or not to accept, the rule in many legal systems is that an offer is irrevocable unless it provides otherwise. The common-law rule, on the other hand, resting on the requirement of consideration, permits the revocation of offers even though stated to be firm. See Comment *a* to § 42. The offeree's need for a dependable basis for decision is met in part by the common-law rule that mailed acceptance prevents a revocation. See § 63. Where more is needed, the option contract is available.

d. Effect of option contract. The principal legal consequence of an option contract is that stated in this Section: it limits the promisor's power to revoke an offer. The termination of the offeree's power of acceptance is subject to the requirements for discharge of a contractual duty. See § 37. A revocation by the offeror is not of itself effective, and the offer is properly referred to as an irrevocable offer.

§ 26. Preliminary Negotiations

A manifestation of willingness to enter into a bargain is not an offer if the person to whom it is addressed knows or has reason to know that the person making it does not intend to conclude a bargain until he has made a further manifestation of assent.

Comment:

b. Advertising. Business enterprises commonly secure general publicity for the goods or services they supply or purchase. Advertisements of goods by display, sign, handbill, newspaper, radio or television are not ordinarily intended or understood as offers to sell. The same is true of catalogues, price lists and circulars, even though the terms of suggested bargains may be stated in some detail. It is of course possible to make an offer by an advertisement directed to the general public (see § 29), but there must ordinarily be some language of commitment or some invitation to take action without further communication.

c. Quotation of price. A "quotation" of price is usually a statement of price per unit of quantity; it may omit the quantity to be sold, time and place of delivery, terms of payment, and other terms. It is sometimes associated with a price list or circular, but the word "quote" is commonly understood as inviting an offer rather than as making one, even when directed to a particular customer. But just as the word "offer" does not necessarily mean that an offer is intended, so the word "quote" may be used in an offer. In determining whether an offer is made relevant factors include the terms of any previous inquiry, the completeness of the terms of the suggested bargain, and the number of persons to whom a communication is addressed.

d. Invitation of bids or other offers. Even though terms are specified in detail, it is common for one party to request the other to make an offer. The words "Make me an offer" would normally indicate that no offer is being made, and other conduct such as the announcement of an auction may have similar effect. See § 28. A request for bids on a construction project is similar, even though the practice may be to accept the lowest bid conforming to specifications and other requirements. And forms used or statements made by a traveling salesman may make it clear that the customer is making an offer to be accepted at the salesman's home office. See § 69.

§ 27. Existence of Contract Where Written Memorial Is Contemplated

Manifestations of assent that are in themselves sufficient to conclude a contract will not be prevented from so operating by the fact that the parties also manifest an intention to prepare and adopt a written memorial thereof; but the circumstances may show that the agreements are preliminary negotiations.

§ 28. Auctions

(1) At an auction, unless a contrary intention is manifested,

(a) the auctioneer invites offers from successive bidders which he may accept or reject;

(b) when goods are put up without reserve, the auctioneer makes an offer to sell at any price bid by the highest bidder, and after the auctioneer calls for bids the goods cannot be withdrawn unless no bid is made within a reasonable time;

(c) whether or not the auction is without reserve, a bidder may withdraw his bid until the auctioneer's announcement of completion of the sale, but a bidder's retraction does not revive any previous bid.

(2) Unless a contrary intention is manifested, bids at an auction embody terms made known by advertisement, posting or other publication of which bidders are or should be aware, as modified by any announcement made by the auctioneer when the goods are put up.

Illustration:

1. A publishes an advertisement saying that he will sell his household goods at public auction at a specific time and place. This in no way affects his legal relations.

§ 29. To Whom an Offer Is Addressed

(1) The manifested intention of the offeror determines the person or persons in whom is created a power of acceptance.

(2) An offer may create a power of acceptance in a specified person or in one or more of a specified group or class of persons, acting separately or

together, or in anyone or everyone who makes a specified promise or renders a specified performance.

Comment:

a. Terms of offer control. The rule stated in Subsection (1) is an elaboration of the definition of offer in § 24, and it is to be read in the light of the rules stated §§ 23 and 26. The offeror is the master of his offer; just as the making of any offer at all can be avoided by appropriate language or other conduct, so the power of acceptance can be narrowly limited. The offeror is bound only in accordance with his manifested assent; he is not bound just because he receives a consideration as good as or better than the one he bargained for. But if he knows or has reason to know that he is creating an appearance of assent, he may be bound by that appearance. These considerations apply to the identity of the offeree or offerees as well as to the mode of manifesting acceptance (see § 30) and the substance of the exchange (see §§ 31, 32, 58).

§ 30. Form of Acceptance Invited

(1) An offer may invite or require acceptance to be made by an affirmative answer in words, or by performing or refraining from performing a specified act, or may empower the offeree to make a selection of terms in his acceptance.

(2) Unless otherwise indicated by the language or the circumstances, an offer invites acceptance in any manner and by any medium reasonable in the circumstances.

Comment:

a. Required form. The offeror is the master of his offer. See Comment *a* to § 29. The form of acceptance is less likely to affect the substance of the bargain than the identity of the offeree, and is often quite immaterial. But the offeror is entitled to insist on a particular mode of manifestation of assent. The terms of the offer may limit acceptance to a particular mode; whether it does so is a matter of interpretation.

Illustration:

1. A sends a letter to B stating the terms of a proposed contract. At the end he writes, "You can accept this offer only by signing on the dotted line below my own signature." A replies by telegram, "I accept your offer." There is no contract.

§ 31. Offer Proposing a Single Contract or a Number of Contracts

An offer may propose the formation of a single contract by a single acceptance or the formation of a number of contracts by successive acceptances from time to time.

§ 32. Invitation of Promise or Performance

In case of doubt an offer is interpreted as inviting the offeree to accept either by promising to perform what the offer requests or by rendering the performance, as the offeree chooses.

§ 33. Certainty

(1) Even though a manifestation of intention is intended to be understood as an offer, it cannot be accepted so as to form a contract unless the terms of the contract are reasonably certain.

(2) The terms of a contract are reasonably certain if they provide a basis for determining the existence of a breach and for giving an appropriate remedy.

(3) The fact that one or more terms of a proposed bargain are left open or uncertain may show that a manifestation of intention is not intended to be understood as an offer or as an acceptance.

§ 34. Certainty and Choice of Terms; Effect of Performance or Reliance

(1) The terms of a contract may be reasonably certain even though it empowers one or both parties to make a selection of terms in the course of performance.

(2) Part performance under an agreement may remove uncertainty and establish that a contract enforceable as a bargain has been formed.

(3) Action in reliance on an agreement may make a contractual remedy appropriate even though uncertainty is not removed.

TOPIC 4. DURATION OF THE OFFEREE'S POWER OF ACCEPTANCE

§ 35 The Offeree's Power of Acceptance

(1) An offer gives the offeree a continuing power to complete the manifestation of mutual assent by acceptance of the offer.

(2) A contract cannot be created by acceptance of an offer after the power of acceptance has been terminated in one of the ways listed in § 36.

§36. Methods of Termination of the Power of Acceptance

(1) An offeree's power of acceptance may be terminated by
 (a) rejection or counter-offer by the offeree, or
 (b) lapse of time, or
 (c) revocation by the offeror, or
 (d) death or incapacity of the offeror or offeree.
(2) In addition, an offeree's power of acceptance is terminated by the non-occurrence of any condition of acceptance under the terms of the offer.

§37. Termination of Power of Acceptance Under Option Contract

Notwithstanding §§38-49, the power of acceptance under an option contract is not terminated by rejection or counter-offer, by revocation, or by death or incapacity of the offeror, unless the requirements are met for the discharge of a contractual duty.

§38. Rejection

(1) An offeree's power of acceptance is terminated by his rejection of the offer, unless the offeror has manifested a contrary intention.

(2) A manifestation of intention not to accept an offer is a rejection unless the offeree manifests an intention to take it under further advisement.

§39. Counter-Offers

(1) A counter-offer is an offer made by an offeree to his offeror relating to the same matter as the original offer and proposing a substituted bargain differing from that proposed by the original offer.

(2) An offeree's power of acceptance is terminated by his making of a counter-offer, unless the offeror has manifested a contrary intention or unless the counter-offer manifests a contrary intention of the offeree.

Illustration:

1. A offers to B to sell him a parcel of land for $5,000, stating that the offer will remain open for thirty days. B replies, "I will pay $4,800.00 for the parcel," and on A's declining that, B writes, within the thirty day period, "I accept your offer to sell for $5,000." There is no contract unless A's offer was itself a contract (see §37), or unless A's reply to the counter-offer manifested an intention to renew his original offer.

Comment:

b. Qualified acceptance, inquiry or separate offer. A common type of counter-offer is the qualified or conditional acceptance, which purports to accept the original offer but makes acceptance expressly conditional on assent to additional or different terms. See § 59. Such a counter-offer must be distinguished from an unqualified acceptance which is accompanied by a proposal for modification of the agreement or for a separate agreement. A mere inquiry regarding the possibility of different terms, a request for a better offer, or a comment upon the terms of the offer, is ordinarily not a counter-offer. Such responses to an offer may be too tentative or indefinite to be offers of any kind; or they may deal with new matters rather than a substitution for the original offer; or their language may manifest an intention to keep the original offer under consideration.

Illustrations:

2. A makes the same offer to B as that stated in Illustration 1, and B replies, "Won't you take less?" A answers, "No." An acceptance thereafter by B within the thirty-day period is effective. B's inquiry was not a counter-offer, and A's original offer stands.

3. A makes the same offer to B as that stated in Illustration 1. B replies, "I am keeping your offer under advisement, but if you wish to close the matter at once I will give you $4,800." A does not reply, and within the thirty-day period B accepts the original offer. B's acceptance is effective.

§ 40. Time When Rejection or Counter-Offer Terminates the Power of Acceptance

Rejection or counter-offer by mail or telegram does not terminate the power of acceptance until received by the offeror, but limits the power so that a letter or telegram of acceptance started after the sending of an otherwise effective rejection or counter-offer is only a counter-offer unless the acceptance is received by the offeror before he receives the rejection or counter-offer.

Comment:

b. Subsequent acceptance. Since a rejection of counter-offer is not effective until received, it may until that time be superseded by an acceptance. But the probability remains that the offeror will rely on the rejection or counter-offer if it is received before the acceptance. To protect the offeror in such reliance, the offeree who has dispatched a rejection is deprived of the benefit of the rule that an acceptance may take effect on dispatch (§ 63). . . .

Illustration:

1. A makes B an offer by mail. B immediately after receiving the offer mails a letter of rejection. Within the time permitted by the offer B accepts. This acceptance creates a contract only if received before the rejection, or if the power of acceptance continues under §§ 37-39.

§41. Lapse of Time

(1) An offeree's power of acceptance is terminated at the time specified in the offer, or, if no time is specified, at the end of a reasonable time.

(2) What is a reasonable time is a question of fact, depending on all the circumstances existing when the offer and attempted acceptance are made.

Comment:

b. Reasonable time. In the absence of a contrary indication, just as acceptance may be made in any manner and by any medium which is reasonable in the circumstances (§30), so it may be made at any time which is reasonable in the circumstances. The circumstances to be considered have a wide range; they include the nature of the proposed contract, the purposes of the parties, the course of dealing between them, and any relevant usages of trade. In general, the question is what time would be thought satisfactory to the offeror by a reasonable man in the position of the offeree; but circumstances not known to the offeree may be relevant to show that the time actually taken by the offeree was satisfactory to the offeror.

d. Direct negotiations. Where the parties bargain face to face or over the telephone, the time for acceptance does not ordinarily extend beyond the end of the conversation unless a contrary intention is indicated. . . .

e. Offers made by mail or telegram. Where the parties are at a distance from each other, the normal understanding is that the time for acceptance is extended at least by the normal time for transmission of the offer and for the sending of the offeree's reply.

f. Speculative transactions. The reasonable time for acceptance in a speculative transaction is brief not only because the offeror does not ordinarily intend to assume an extended risk without compensation but also because he does not intend to give the offeree an extended opportunity for speculation at the offeror's expense.

Illustration:

8. A sends B an offer by mail to sell at a fixed price corporate stock not listed on an exchange. B waits two days after receiving the offer and then sends a telegraphic acceptance after learning of a sharp rise in the price bid over-the-counter. The acceptance may be too late even though it arrives before a prompt acceptance by mail would have arrived.

§42. Revocation by Communication from Offeror Received by Offeree

An offeree's power of acceptance is terminated when the offeree receives from the offeror a manifestation of an intention not to enter into the proposed contract.

Comment:

a. Revocability of offers. Most offers are revocable. Revocability may rest on the express or implied terms of the offer, as in the case of bids at an auction. See § 28. But the ordinary offer is revocable even though it expressly states the contrary, because of the doctrine that an informal agreement is binding as a bargain only if supported by consideration. Inroads have been made on that doctrine by statute and by rules giving effect to nominal consideration and to action in reliance on a promise. Where such rules are applicable, or where the offer is itself a formal contract or an agreement binding as a bargain, the case is governed by § 37 rather than by this Section. See § 25.

Illustration:

1. A makes a written offer to B to sell him a piece of land. The offer states that it will remain open for thirty days and is not subject to countermand. The next day A orally informs B that the offer is terminated. B's power of acceptance is terminated unless the offer is a contract under § 25.

b. Necessity that communication be received. An offeror may reserve the power to revoke the offer without notice, and such a reservation will be given effect whether contained in the offer or in a later communication received by the offeree before a contract is created. But such a reservation is unusual; it deprives the offeree of a dependable basis for decision whether to accept and greatly impairs the usefulness of the offer. In the absence of such a reservation, the offeree is justified in relying on the offeror's manifested intention regardless of any undisclosed change in the offeror's state of mind. As to when a revocation is received by the offeree, see § 68; compare . . . Uniform Commercial Code § 1-201[(36)].

c. Purported revocation after acceptance. Once the offeree has exercised his power to create a contract by accepting the offer, a purported revocation is ineffective as such. Where an acceptance by mail is effective on dispatch, for example, it is not deprived of effect by a revocation subsequently received by the offeree. See § 63. But the revocation may have effect, depending on its terms, as a failure of condition discharging the offeree's duty of performance, as a breach by anticipatory repudiation, or as an offer to modify or rescind the contract.

d. What constitutes revocation. The word "revoke" is not essential to a revocation. Any clear manifestation of unwillingness to enter into the proposed bargain is sufficient. Thus a statement that property offered for sale has been otherwise disposed of is a revocation. But equivocal language may not be sufficient.

§ 43. Indirect Communication of Revocation

An offeree's power of acceptance is terminated when the offeror takes definite action inconsistent with an intention to enter into the proposed contract and the offeree acquires reliable information to that effect.

§ 44. Effect of Deposit on Revocability of Offer

An offeror's power of revocation is not limited by the deposit of money or other property to be forfeited in the event of revocation, but the deposit may be forfeited to the extent that it is not a penalty.

§45. Option Contract Created by Part Performance or Tender

(1) Where an offer invites an offeree to accept by rendering a performance and does not invite a promissory acceptance, an option contract is created when the offeree tenders or begins the invited performance or tenders a beginning of it.

(2) The offeror's duty of performance under any option contract so created is conditional on completion or tender of the invited performance in accordance with the terms of the offer.

Comment:

b. Manifestation of contrary intention. The rule of this Section is designed to protect the offeree in justifiable reliance on the offeror's promise, and the rule yields to a manifestation of intention which makes reliance justified.

§46. Revocation of General Offer

Where an offer is made by advertisement in a newspaper or other general notification to the public or to a number of persons whose identity is unknown to the offeror, the offeree's power of acceptance is terminated when a notice of termination is given publicity by advertisement or other general notification equal to that given to the offer and no better means of notification is reasonably available.

§47. Revocation of Divisible Offer

An offer contemplating a series of independent contracts by separate acceptances may be effectively revoked so as to terminate the power to create future contracts, though one or more of the proposed contracts have already been formed by the offeree's acceptance.

§48. Death or Incapacity of Offeror or Offeree

An offeree's power of acceptance is terminated when the offeree or offeror dies or is deprived of legal capacity to enter into the proposed contract.

Comment:

a. Death of offeror. The offeror's death terminates the power of the offeree without notice to him. This rule seems to be a relic of the obsolete view that a contract requires a "meeting of minds," and it is out of harmony with the modern doctrine that a manifestation of assent is effective without regard to actual mental assent. See § 19. . . .

c. Death or incapacity of offeree. Only the offeree can accept an offer which is not also a contract. See § 52. When the offeree dies or lacks capacity, therefore, acceptance is impossible. Compare Comment *b* to § 36. By the terms of the offer, however, the personal representative or distributee of the offeree may be made an additional offeree.

d. Option contracts. The rule stated in this Section does not affect option contracts. See § 37. But the death or incapacity of one of the parties may discharge any contractual duty by reason of failure of consideration, frustration, impossibility or failure of condition. See § 36 and Comment.

§ 49. Effect of Delay in Communication of Offer

If communication of an offer to the offeree is delayed, the period within which a contract can be created by acceptance is not thereby extended if the offeree knows or has reason to know of the delay, though it is due to the fault of the offeror; but if the delay is due to the fault of the offeror or to the means of transmission adopted by him, and the offeree neither knows nor has reason to know that there has been delay, a contract can be created by acceptance within the period which would have been permissible if the offer had been dispatched at the time that its arrival seems to indicate.

TOPIC 5. ACCEPTANCE OF OFFERS

§ 50. Acceptance of Offer Defined; Acceptance by Performance; Acceptance by Promise

(1) Acceptance of an offer is a manifestation of assent to the terms thereof made by the offeree in a manner invited or required by the offer.

(2) Acceptance by performance requires that at least part of what the offer requests be performed or tendered and includes acceptance by a performance which operates as a return promise.

(3) Acceptance by a promise requires that the offeree complete every act essential to the making of the promise.

§ 51. Effect of Part Performance Without Knowledge of Offer

Unless the offeror manifests a contrary intention, an offeree who learns of an offer after he has rendered part of the performance requested by the offer may accept by completing the requested performance.

§52. Who May Accept an Offer

An offer can be accepted only by a person whom it invites to furnish the consideration.

§53. Acceptance by Performance; Manifestation of Intention Not to Accept

(1) An offer can be accepted by the rendering of a performance only if the offer invites such an acceptance.

(2) Except as stated in §69, the rendering of a performance does not constitute an acceptance if within a reasonable time the offeree exercises reasonable diligence to notify the offeror of non-acceptance.

(3) Where an offer of a promise invites acceptance by performance and does not invite a promissory acceptance, the rendering of the invited performance does not constitute an acceptance if before the offeror performs his promise the offeree manifests an intention not to accept.

§54. Acceptance by Performance; Necessity of Notification to Offeror

(1) Where an offer invites an offeree to accept by rendering a performance, no notification is necessary to make such an acceptance effective unless the offer requests such a notification.

(2) If an offeree who accepts by rendering a performance has reason to know that the offeror has no adequate means of learning of the performance with reasonable promptness and certainty, the contractual duty of the offeror is discharged unless

(a) the offeree exercises reasonable diligence to notify the offeror of acceptance, or

(b) the offeror learns of the performance within a reasonable time, or

(c) the offer indicates that notification of acceptance is not required.

Comment:

a. Rationale. In the usual commercial bargain the offeror expects and receives prompt notification of acceptance, and such notification is ordinarily essential to an acceptance by promise. See §56. But where an offer invites the offeree to accept by rendering a performance, the offeree needs a dependable basis for his decision whether to accept. Compare §63 and Comment *a*. When the offeree performs or begins to perform in response to such an offer, there is need for protection of his justifiable reliance. Compare §45. Those needs are met by giving the performance the effect of temporarily barring revocation of the offer; but ordinarily notification of the offeror must follow in due course. See Uniform Commercial Code § 2-206 Comment 3.

§ 55. Acceptance of Non-Promissory Offers

Acceptance by promise may create a contract in which the offeror's performance is completed when the offeree's promise is made.

Comment:

a. "Reverse unilateral contracts." It is possible to offer a performance without making any promise. Like other offers, a non-promissory offer may require acceptance by performance or acceptance by promise or a combination of the two, or it may leave the mode of acceptance to the offeree's choice. An exchange of performances is not within the definition of "contract" in § 1 and is beyond the scope of the Restatement of this Subject. But where a non-promissory offer is accepted by promise, there is a contract if the requirements other than manifestation of mutual assent are met. Since the contract formed by a performance in response to an offer of a promise such as an offer of reward is often called a "unilateral contract," the type of contract referred to in this Section is sometimes referred to as a "reverse unilateral contract." Contracts so referred to often involve incidental promises by the performing offeror, and in that event the word "unilateral" is not entirely appropriate.

§ 56. Acceptance by Promise; Necessity of Notification to Offeror

Except as stated in § 69 or where the offer manifests a contrary intention, it is essential to an acceptance by promise either that the offeree exercise reasonable diligence to notify the offeror of acceptance or that the offeror receive the acceptance seasonably.

§ 57. Effect of Equivocal Acceptance

Where notification is essential to acceptance by promise, the offeror is not bound by an acceptance in equivocal terms unless he reasonably understands it as an acceptance.

§ 58. Necessity of Acceptance Complying with Terms of Offer

An acceptance must comply with the requirements of the offer as to the promise to be made or the performance to be rendered.

Comment:

a. Scope. This rule applies to the substance of the bargain the basic principle that the offeror is the master of his offer. See Comment a to § 29. That principle rests on the concept of private autonomy underlying contract law. It is mitigated by the interpretation of offers, in accordance with common understanding, as inviting acceptance in any reasonable manner unless there is a contrary indication. See §§ 20, 30(2), 32. Usage of trade or course of dealing may permit inconsequential variations; or a variation clearly to the offeror's advantage, such as a reduction in the price of ordered goods, may be within the scope of the offer. But even in such cases the offeror is entitled, if he makes his meaning clear, to insist on a prescribed type of acceptance.

Illustrations:

1. A offers to sell a book to B for $5 and states that no other acceptance will be honored but the mailing of B's personal check for exactly $5. B personally tenders $5 in legal tender, or mails a personal check for $10. There is no contract.

2. A offers to pay B $100 for plowing Flodden field, and states that acceptance is to be made only by posting a letter before beginning work and before the next Monday noon. Before Monday noon B completes the requested plowing and mails to A a letter stating that the work is complete. There is no contract.

§ 59. Purported Acceptance Which Adds Qualifications

A reply to an offer which purports to accept it but is conditional on the offeror's assent to terms additional to or different from those offered is not an acceptance but is a counter-offer.

Comment:

a. Qualified acceptance. A qualified conditional acceptance proposes an exchange different from that proposed by the original offeror. Such a proposal is a counter-offer and ordinarily terminates the power of acceptance of the original offeree. See § 39. The effect of the qualification or condition is to deprive the purported acceptance of effect. But a definite and seasonable expression of acceptance is operative despite the statement of additional or different terms if the acceptance is not made to depend on assent to the additional or different terms. See § 61; Uniform Commercial Code § 2-207(1). The additional or different terms are then to be construed as proposals for modification of the contract. See Uniform Commercial Code § 2-207(2). Such proposals may sometimes be accepted by the silence of the original offeror. See § 69.

Illustration:

1. A makes an offer to B, and B in terms accepts but adds, "This acceptance is not effective unless prompt acknowledgement is made of receipt of this letter." There is no contract, but a counter-offer.

§ 60. Acceptance of Offer Which States Place, Time or Manner of Acceptance

If an offer prescribes the place, time or manner of acceptance its terms in this respect must be complied with in order to create a contract. If an offer merely suggests a permitted place, time or manner of acceptance, another method of acceptance is not precluded.

Comment:

a. Interpretation of offer. If the offeror prescribes the only way in which his offer may be accepted, an acceptance in any other way is a counter-offer. But frequently in regard to the details of methods of acceptance, the offeror's language, if fairly interpreted, amounts merely to a statement of a satisfactory method of acceptance, without positive requirement that this method shall be followed.

Illustrations:

1. A mails an offer to B in which A says, "I must receive your acceptance by return mail." An acceptance sent within a reasonable time by any other means, which reaches A as soon as a letter sent by return mail would normally arrive, creates a contract on arrival. As to what is a reasonable time, see Illustration 8 to § 41.

2. A makes an offer to B and adds, "Send your office boy around with an answer to this by twelve o'clock." The offeree comes himself before twelve o'clock and accepts. There is a contract.

3. A offers to sell his land to B on certain terms, also saying: "You must accept this, if at all, in person at my office at ten o'clock tomorrow." B's power is strictly limited to one method of acceptance.

§ 61. Acceptance Which Requests Change of Terms

An acceptance which requests a change or addition to the terms of the offer is not thereby invalidated unless the acceptance is made to depend on an assent to the changed or added terms.

Comment:

a. Interpretation of acceptance. An acceptance must be unequivocal. But the mere inclusion of words requesting a modification of the proposed terms does not prevent a purported acceptance from closing the contract unless, if fairly interpreted, the offeree's assent depends on the offeror's further acquiescence in the modification. See Uniform Commercial Code § 2-207(1).

Illustration:

1. A offers to sell B 100 tons of steel at a certain price. B replies, "I accept your offer. I hope that if you can arrange to deliver the steel in weekly installments of 25 tons you will do so." There is a contract, but A is not bound to deliver in installments.

§ 62. Effect of Performance by Offeree Where Offer Invites Either Performance or Promise

(1) Where an offer invites an offeree to choose between acceptance by promise and acceptance by performance, the tender or beginning of the invited performance or a tender of a beginning of it is an acceptance by performance.

(2) Such an acceptance operates as a promise to render complete performance.

Comment:

d. Preparations for performance. As under § 45, what is begun or tendered must be part of the actual performance invited, rather than preparation for performance, in order to make the rule of this Section applicable. But preparations to perform may bring the case within § 87(2) on justifiable reliance.

Illustrations:

1. A, a merchant, mails B, a carpenter in the same city, an offer to employ B to fit up A's office in accordance with A's specifications and B's estimate previously submitted, the work to be completed in two weeks. The offer says, "You may begin at once," and B immediately buys the lumber and begins to work on it in his own shop. The next day, before B has sent a notice of acceptance or begun work at A's office or rendered the lumber unfit for other jobs, A revokes the offer. The revocation is timely, since B has not begun to perform.

2. A, a regular customer of B, orders fragile goods from B which B carries in stock and ships in his own trucks. Following his usual practice, B selects the goods ordered, tags them as A's, crates them and loads them on a truck at substantial expense. Performance has begun and A's offer is irrevocable. See Uniform Commercial Code § 2-206 and Comment 2.

§ 63. Time When Acceptance Takes Effect

Unless the offer provides otherwise,

(a) an acceptance made in a manner and by a medium invited by an offer is operative and completes the manifestation of mutual assent as soon as put out of the offeree's possession, without regard to whether it ever reaches the offeror; but

(b) an acceptance under an option contract is not operative until received by the offeror.

Comment:

a. Rationale. It is often said that an offeror who makes an offer by mail makes the post office his agent to receive the acceptance, or that the mailing of a letter of acceptance puts it irrevocably out of the offeree's control. Under United States postal regulations, however, the sender of a letter has long had the power to stop delivery and reclaim the letter. A better explanation of the rule that the acceptance takes effect on dispatch is that the offeree needs a dependable basis for his decision whether to accept. In many legal systems such a basis is provided by a general rule that an offer is irrevocable unless it provides otherwise. The common law provides such a basis through the rule that a revocation of an offer is ineffective if received after an acceptance has been properly dispatched. See Comment *c* to § 42. Acceptance by telegram is governed in this respect by the same considerations as acceptance by mail.

Illustration:

1. A makes B an offer, inviting acceptance by telegram, and B duly telegraphs an acceptance. A purports to revoke the offer in person or by telephone or telegraph, but the attempted revocation is received by B after the telegram of acceptance is dispatched. There is no effective revocation.

c. Revocation of acceptance. The fact that the offeree has power to reclaim his acceptance from the post office or telegraph company does not prevent the acceptance from taking effect on dispatch. Nor, in the absence of additional circumstances, does the actual recapture of the acceptance deprive it of legal effect, though as a practical matter the offeror cannot assert his rights unless he learns of them. An attempt to revoke the acceptance by an overtaking communication is similarly ineffective, even though the revocation is received before the acceptance is received. After mailing an acceptance of a revocable offer, the offeree is not permitted to speculate at the offeror's expense during the time required for the letter to arrive.

A purported revocation of acceptance may, however, affect the rights of the parties. It may amount to an offer to rescind the contract or to a repudiation of it, or it may bar the offeree by estoppel from enforcing it. In some cases it may be justified as an exercise of a right of stoppage in transit or a demand for assurance of performance. . . . Or the contract may be voidable for mistake or misrepresentation, §§ 151-54, 164. See particularly the provisions of § 153 on unilateral mistake.

§ 64. Acceptance by Telephone or Teletype

Acceptance given by telephone or other medium of substantially instantaneous two-way communication is governed by the principles applicable to acceptances where the parties are in the presence of each other.

§65. Reasonableness of Medium of Acceptance

Unless circumstances known to the offeree indicate otherwise, a medium of acceptance is reasonable if it is the one used by the offeror or one customary in similar transactions at the time and place the offer is received.

Comment:

b. Circumstances relevant to reasonableness. This Section specifies certain circumstances which ordinarily indicate that a particular medium of acceptance is reasonable, but it does not exhaust the circumstances which may be relevant. Among the relevant circumstances not specified in this Section may be the speed and reliability of the medium, a prior course of dealing between the parties, and a usage of trade. See Chapter 9. The concept of reasonableness is flexible, and its applicability may be enlarged as new media develop or existing media become more speedy or reliable or come into more general use. See Comment 1 to Uniform Commercial Code §2-206.

§66. Acceptance Must Be Properly Dispatched

An acceptance sent by mail or otherwise from a distance is not operative when dispatched, unless it is properly addressed and such other precautions taken as are ordinarily observed to insure safe transmission of similar messages.

§67. Effect of Receipt of Acceptance Improperly Dispatched

Where an acceptance is seasonably dispatched but the offeree uses a means of transmission not invited by the offer or fails to exercise reasonable diligence to insure safe transmission, it is treated as operative upon dispatch if received within the time in which a properly dispatched acceptance would normally have arrived.

§68. What Constitutes Receipt of Revocation, Rejection, or Acceptance

A written revocation, rejection, or acceptance is received when the writing comes into the possession of the person addressed, or of some person authorized by him to receive it for him, or when it is deposited in some place which he has authorized as the place for this or similar communications to be deposited for him.

§ 69. Acceptance by Silence or Exercise of Dominion

(1) Where an offeree fails to reply to an offer, his silence and inaction operate as an acceptance in the following cases only:

(a) Where an offeree takes the benefit of offered services with reasonable opportunity to reject them and reason to know that they were offered with the expectation of compensation.

(b) Where the offeror has stated or given the offeree reason to understand that assent may be manifested by silence or inaction, and the offeree in remaining silent and inactive intends to accept the offer.

(c) Where because of previous dealings or otherwise, it is reasonable that the offeree should notify the offeror if he does not intend to accept.

(2) An offeree who does any act inconsistent with the offeror's ownership of offered property is bound in accordance with the offered terms unless they are manifestly unreasonable. But if the act is wrongful as against the offeror it is an acceptance only if ratified by him.

Comment:

a. Acceptance by silence is exceptional. Ordinarily an offeror does not have power to cause the silence of the offeree to operate as acceptance. See Comment *b* to § 53. The usual requirement of notification is stated in § 54 on acceptance by performance and § 56 on acceptance by promise. The mere receipt of an unsolicited offer does not impair the offeree's freedom of action or inaction or impose on him any duty to speak. The exceptional cases where silence is acceptance fall into two main classes: those where the offeree silently takes offered benefits, and those where one party relies on the other party's manifestation of intention that silence may operate as acceptance. Even in those cases the contract may be unenforceable under the Statute of Frauds. See Chapter 5.

d. Prior conduct of the offeree. Explicit statement by the offeree, usage of trade, or a course of dealing between the parties may give the offeror reason to understand that silence will constitute acceptance. In such a situation the offer may tacitly incorporate that understanding, and if the offeree intends to accept the case then falls within Subsection (1)(b). Under Subsection (1)(c) the offeree's silence is acceptance, regardless of his actual intent, unless both parties understand that no acceptance is intended. See § 20. . . .

§ 70. Effect of Receipt by Offeror of a Late or Otherwise Defective Acceptance

A late or otherwise defective acceptance may be effective as an offer to the original offeror, but his silence operates as an acceptance in such a case only as stated in § 69.

CHAPTER 4 FORMATION OF CONTRACTS—CONSIDERATION

TOPIC 1. THE REQUIREMENT OF CONSIDERATION

§71. Requirement of Exchange; Types of Exchange

(1) To constitute consideration, a performance or a return promise must be bargained for.

(2) A performance or return promise is bargained for if it is sought by the promisor in exchange for his promise and is given by the promisee in exchange for that promise.

(3) The performance may consist of
  (a) an act other than a promise, or
  (b) a forbearance, or
  (c) the creation, modification, or destruction of a legal relation.

(4) The performance or return promise may be given to the promisor or to some other person. It may be given by the promisee or by some other person.

Comment:

a. Other meanings of "consideration." The word "consideration" has often been used with meanings different from that given here. It is often used merely to express the legal conclusion that a promise is enforceable. Historically, its primary meaning may have been that the conditions were met under which an action of assumpsit would lie. It was also used as the equivalent of the quid pro quo required in an action of debt. A seal, it has been said, "imports a consideration," although the law was clear that no element of bargain was necessary to enforcement of a promise under seal. On the other hand, consideration has sometimes been used to refer to almost any reason asserted for enforcing a promise, even though the reason was insufficient. In this sense we find references to promises "in consideration of love and affection," to "illegal consideration," to "past consideration," and to consideration furnished by reliance on a gratuitous promise.

Consideration has also been used to refer to the element of exchange without regard to legal consequences. Consistent with that usage has been the use of the phrase "sufficient consideration" to express the legal conclusion that one requirement for an enforceable bargain is met. Here § 17 states the element of exchange required for a contract enforceable as a bargain as "a consideration." Thus "consideration" refers to an element of exchange which is sufficient to satisfy the legal requirement; the word "sufficient" would be redundant and is not used.

b. "Bargained for." In the typical bargain, the consideration and the promise bear a reciprocal relation of motive or inducement: the consideration induces the making of the promise and the promise induces the furnishing of the consideration. Here, as in the matter of mutual assent, the law is concerned with the external manifestation rather than the undisclosed mental state: it is enough that one party manifests an intention to induce the other's response and to be induced by it and that the other responds in accordance with the inducement. See § 81; compare §§ 19, 20. But it is not enough that the promise induces the conduct of the promisee or that the conduct of the promisee induces the making of the promise; both elements must be present, or there is no bargain. Moreover, a mere pretense of bargain does not suffice, as where there is a false recital of consideration or where the purported consideration is merely nominal. In such cases there is no consideration and the promise is enforced, if at all, as a promise binding without consideration under §§ 82-94. See Comments *b* and *c* to § 87.

Illustrations:

1. A offers to buy a book owned by B and to pay B $10 in exchange therefor. B accepts the offer and delivers the book to A. The transfer and delivery of the book constitute a performance and are consideration for A's promise. See Uniform Commercial Code §§ 2-106, 2-301. This is so even though A at the time he makes the offer secretly intends to pay B $10 whether or not he gets the book, or even though B at the time he accepts secretly intends not to collect the $10.

2. A receives a gift from B of a book worth $10. Subsequently A promises to pay B the value of the book. There is no consideration for A's promise. This is so even though B at the time he makes the gift secretly hopes that A will pay him for it. As to the enforcement of such promises, see § 86.

3. A promises to make a gift of $10 to B. In reliance on the promise B buys a book from C and promises to pay C $10 for it. There is no consideration for A's promise. As to the enforcement of such promises, see § 90.

c. Mixture of bargain and gift. In most commercial bargains there is a rough equivalence between the value promised and the value received as consideration. But the social functions of bargains include the provision of opportunity for free individual action and exercise of judgment and the fixing of values by private action, either generally or for purposes of the particular transaction. Those functions would be impaired by judicial review of the values so fixed. Ordinarily, therefore, courts do not inquire into the adequacy of consideration, particularly where one or both of the values exchanged are difficult to measure. See § 79. Even where both parties know that a transaction is in part a bargain and in part a gift, the element of bargain may nevertheless furnish consideration for the entire transaction.

On the other hand, a gift is not ordinarily treated as a bargain, and a promise to make a gift is not made a bargain by the promise of the prospective donee to accept the gift, or by his acceptance of part of it. This may be true even though the terms of gift impose a burden on the donee as well as the donor. . . . In such cases the distinction between bargain and gift may be a fine one, depending on the motives manifested by the parties. In some cases there may be no bargain so long as the agreement is entirely executory, but performance may furnish consideration or the agreement may become fully or partly enforceable by virtue of the reliance of one party or the unjust enrichment of the other. Compare § 90.

Illustration:

6. A offers to buy a book owned by B and to pay B $10 in exchange therefor. B's transfer and delivery of the book are consideration for A's promise even though both parties know that such books regularly sell for $5 and that part of A's motive in making the offer is to make a gift to B. See §§ 79, 81.

d. Types of consideration. Consideration may consist of a performance or of a return promise. Consideration by way of performance may be a specified act of forbearance, or any one of several specified acts or forbearances of which the offeree is given the choice, or such conduct as will produce a specified result. Or either the offeror or the offeree may request as consideration the creation, modification or destruction of a purely intangible legal relation. Not infrequently the consideration bargained for is an act with the added requirement that a certain legal result shall be produced. Consideration by way of return promise requires a promise as defined in § 2. Consideration may consist partly of promise and partly of other acts or forbearances, and the consideration invited may be a performance or a return promise in the alternative. Though a promise is itself an act, it is treated separately from other acts. See § 75[.]

e. Consideration moving from or to a third person. It matters not from whom the consideration moves or to whom it goes. If it is bargained for and given in exchange for the promise, the promise is not gratuitous.

Illustrations:

14. A promises to guarantee payment of a bill of goods if B sells the goods to C. Selling the goods to C is consideration for A's promise.

15. A makes a promissory note payable to B in return for a payment by B to C. The payment is consideration for the note.

§ 72. Exchange of Promise for Performance

Except as stated in §§ 73 and 74, any performance which is bargained for is consideration.

Comment:

b. Substantive bases for enforcement; the half-completed exchange. Bargains are widely believed to be beneficial to the community in the provision of opportunities for freedom of individual action and exercise of judgment and as a means by which productive energy and product are apportioned in the economy. The enforcement of bargains rests in part on the common belief that enforcement enhances that utility. Where one party has performed, there are additional grounds for enforcement. Where, for example, one party has received goods from the other and has broken his promise to pay for them, enforcement of the promise not only encourages the making of socially useful bargains; it also reimburses the seller for a loss incurred in reliance on the promise and prevents the unjust enrichment of the buyer at the seller's expense. Each of these three grounds of enforcement, bargain, reliance and unjust enrichment, has independent force, but the bargain element alone satisfies the requirement of consideration except in the cases covered by §§ 73, 74, 76 and 77. Cases of promises binding by virtue of reliance or unjust enrichment are dealt with in §§ 82-[91].

c. Formality. Consideration furnishes a substantive rather than a formal basis for the enforcement of a promise. Many bargains, particularly when fully performed on one side, involve acts in the course of performance which satisfy some or all of the functions of form and thus may be thought of as natural formalities. Four principal functions have been identified which legal formalities in general may serve: the *evidentiary* function, to provide evidence of the existence and terms of the contract; the *cautionary* function, to guard the promisor against ill-considered action; the *deterrent* function, to discourage transactions of doubtful utility; and the *channeling* or signalizing function, to distinguish a particular type of transaction from other types and from tentative or exploratory expressions of intention in the way that coinage distinguishes money from other metal. But formality is not essential to consideration; nor does formality supply consideration where the element of exchange is absent. . . .

§ 73. Performance of Legal Duty

Performance of a legal duty owed to a promisor which is neither doubtful nor the subject of honest dispute is not consideration; but a similar performance is consideration if it differs from what was required by the duty in a way which reflects more than a pretense of bargain.

Illustrations:

1. A offers a reward to whoever produces evidence leading to the arrest and conviction of the murderer of B. C produces such evidence in the performance of his duty as a police officer. C's performance is not consideration for A's promise.
2. In Illustration 1, C's duties as a police officer are limited to crimes committed in a particular State, and while on vacation he gathers evidence as to a crime committed elsewhere. C's performance is consideration for the promise.

Comment:

c. Contractual duty to the promisor. Legal remedies for breach of contract ordinarily involve delay and expense and rarely put the promise in fully as good a position as voluntary performance. It is therefore often to a promisee's advantage to offer a bonus to a recalcitrant promisor to induce performance without legal proceedings, and an unscrupulous promisor may threaten breach in order to obtain such a bonus. In extreme cases, a bargain for additional compensation under such circumstances may be voidable for duress. See §§ 175-76. And the lack of social utility in such bargains provides what modern justification there is for the rule that performance of a contractual duty is not consideration for a new promise.

But the rule has not been limited to cases where there was a possibility of unfair pressure, and it has been much criticized as resting on scholastic logic. Slight variations of circumstance are commonly held to take a case out of the rule, particularly where the parties have made an equitable adjustment in the course of performance of a continuing contract, or where an impecunious debtor has paid part of his debt in satisfaction of the whole. See §§ 89, 273[.] And in some states the rule has simply been repudiated.

Illustrations:

4. A, an architect, agrees with B to superintend a construction project for a fixed fee. During the course of the project, without excuse, A takes away his plans and refuses to continue, and B promises him an extra fee if A will resume work. A's resumption of work is not consideration for B's promise of an extra fee.

7. A owes B a liquidated sum. Any payment by A at the earlier time, or in a different medium from that required by the duty, is consideration for B's promise to accept it in full satisfaction if the difference in performance is part of what is requested and given in exchange for the promise.

§ 74. Settlement of Claims

(1) Forbearance to assert or the surrender of a claim or defense which proves to be invalid is not consideration unless

(a) the claim or defense is in fact doubtful because of uncertainty as to the facts or the law, or

(b) the forbearing or surrendering party believes that the claim or defense may be fairly determined to be valid.

(2) The execution of a written instrument surrendering a claim or defense by one who is under no duty to execute it is consideration if the execution of the written instrument is bargained for even though he is not asserting the claim or defense and believes that no valid claim or defense exists.

Comment:

b. Requirement of good faith. The policy favoring compromise of disputed claims is clearest, perhaps, where a claim is surrendered at a time when it is uncertain whether it is valid or not. Even though the invalidity later becomes clear, the bargain is to be judged as it appeared to the parties at the time; if the claim was then doubtful, no inquiry is necessary as to their good faith. Even though the invalidity should have been clear at the time, the settlement of an honest dispute is upheld. But a mere assertion or denial of liability does not make a claim doubtful, and the fact that invalidity is obvious may indicate that it was known. In such cases Subsection (1)(b) requires a showing of good faith.

Illustration:

4. A, a real estate broker, is entitled to a commission for selling B's land, amounting to five percent of $300, and offers to pay that amount in full settlement of the claim for commission. A accepts the offer. The payment is consideration for B's promise to surrender his entire claim.

§ 75. Exchange of Promise for Promise

Except as stated in §§ 76 and 77, a promise which is bargained for is consideration if, but only if, the promised performance would be consideration.

§ 76. Conditional Promise

(1) A conditional promise is not consideration if the promisor knows at the time of making the promise that the condition cannot occur.

(2) A promise conditional on a performance by the promisor is a promise of alternative performances within § 77 unless occurrence of the condition is also promised.

§ 77. Illusory and Alternative Promises

A promise or apparent promise is not consideration if by its terms the promisor or purported promisor reserves a choice of alternative performances unless

(a) each of the alternative performances would have been consideration if it alone had been bargained for; or

(b) one of the alternative performances would have been consideration and there is or appears to the parties to be a substantial possibility that before the promisor exercises his choice events may eliminate the alternatives which would not have been consideration.

§ 78. Voidable and Unenforceable Promises

The fact that a rule of law renders a promise voidable or unenforceable does not prevent it from being consideration.

§79. Adequacy of Consideration; Mutuality of Obligation

If the requirement of consideration is met, there is no additional requirement of

(a) a gain, advantage, or benefit to the promisor or a loss, disadvantage, or detriment to the promisee; or

(b) equivalence in the values exchanged; or

(c) "mutuality of obligation."

Comment:

a. Rationale. In such typical bargains as the ordinary sale of goods each party gives up something of economic value, and the values exchanged are often roughly or exactly equivalent by standards independent of the particular bargain. Quite often promise is exchanged for promise, and the promised performances are sometimes divisible into matching parts. See § 31. Hence it has sometimes been said that consideration must consist of a "benefit to the promisor" or a "detriment to the promisee"; it has frequently been claimed that there was no consideration because the economic value given in exchange was much less than that of the promise or the promised performance; "mutuality of obligation" has been said to be essential to a contract. But experience has shown that these are not essential elements of a bargain or of an enforceable contract, and they are negated as requirements by the rules stated in §§ 77-78. This Section makes that negation explicit.

b. Benefit and detriment. Historically, the common law action of debt was said to require a *quid pro quo*, and that requirement may have led to statements that consideration must be a benefit to the promisor. But contracts were enforced in the common-law action of assumpsit without any such requirement; in actions of assumpsit the emphasis was rather on the harm to the promisee, and detrimental reliance on a promise may still be the basis of contractual relief. See § 90. But reliance is not essential to the formation of a bargain, and remedies for breach have long been given in cases of exchange of promise for promise where neither party has begun to perform. Today when it is said that consideration must involve a detriment to the promisee, the supposed requirement is often qualified by a statement that a "legal detriment" is sufficient even though there is no economic detriment or other actual loss. It is more realistic to say simply that there is no requirement of detriment.

Illustration:

1. A contracts to sell property to B. As a favor to B, who is C's friend, and in consideration of A's performance of the contract, C guarantees that B will pay the agreed price. A's performance is consideration for C's promise. See § 73.

d. Pretended exchange. Disparity in value, with or without other circumstances, sometimes indicates that the purported consideration was not in fact bargained for but was a mere formality or pretense. Such a sham of "nominal" consideration does not satisfy the requirement of § 71. Promises are enforced in such cases, if at all, either as promises binding without consideration under §§ 82-[91] or as promises binding by virtue of their formal characteristics under § 6. . . .

§ 80. Multiple Exchanges

(1) There is consideration for a set of promises if what is bargained for and given in exchange would have been consideration for each promise in the set if exchanged for that promise alone.

(2) The fact that part of what is bargained for would not have been consideration if that part alone had been bargained for does not prevent the whole from being consideration.

§ 81. Consideration as Motive or Inducing Cause

(1) The fact that what is bargained for does not itself induce the making of a promise does not prevent it from being consideration for the promise.

(2) The fact that a promise does not of itself induce a performance or return promise does not prevent the performance or return promise from being consideration for the promise.

Comment:

a. "Bargained for." Consideration requires that a performance or return promise be "bargained for" in exchange for a promise; this means that the promisor must manifest an intention to induce the performance or return promise and to be induced by it, and that the promisee must manifest an intention to induce the making of the promise and to be induced by it. See § 71 and Comment *b*. In most commercial bargains the consideration is the object of the promisor's desire and that desire is a material motive or cause inducing the making of the promise, and the reciprocal desire of the promisee for the making of the promise similarly induces the furnishing of the consideration.

b. Immateriality of motive or cause. This Section makes explicit a limitation on the requirement that consideration be bargained for. Even in the typical commercial bargain, the promisor may have more than one motive, and the person furnishing the consideration need not inquire into the promisor's motives. Unless both parties know that the purported consideration is mere pretense, it is immaterial that the promisor's desire for the consideration is incidental to other objectives and even that the other party knows this to be so. Compare § 79 and Illustrations. Subsection (2) states a similar rule with respect to the motives of the promisee.

TOPIC 2. CONTRACTS WITHOUT CONSIDERATION

§82. Promise to Pay Indebtedness; Effect on the Statute of Limitations

(1) A promise to pay all or part of an antecedent contractual or quasi-contractual indebtedness owed by the promisor is binding if the indebtedness is still enforceable or would be except for the effect of a statute of limitations.

(2) The following facts operate as such a promise unless other facts indicate a different intention:

(a) A voluntary acknowledgement to the obligee, admitting the present existence of the antecedent indebtedness; or

(b) A voluntary transfer of money, a negotiable instrument, or other thing by the obligor to the obligee, made as interest on or part payment of or collateral security for the antecedent indebtedness; or

(c) A statement to the obligee that the statute of limitations will not be pleaded as a defense.

Comment:

a. Requirement of a writing. Statutes enacted in most States provide that a promise included in the Section is not binding unless it is in writing and signed by or on behalf of the promisor, except where the promise is inferred from part payment or from the giving of a negotiable instrument or collateral security as stated in Subsection (2)(b). See § 110. In a few States, no writing is required in any case. In a few other States, the rule is more stringent than that generally prevailing and even part payment or giving of security imposes no promissory duty on a debtor unless there is also a signed writing. Most of the statutes requiring a writing are inapplicable to promises supported by consideration or made enforceable by reliance. See § 90.

§83. Promise to Pay Indebtedness Discharged in Bankruptcy

An express promise to pay all or part of an indebtedness of the promisor, discharged or dischargeable in bankruptcy proceedings begun before the promise is made, is binding.

Comment:

a. Rationale. The early history of the rule of this Section is the same as that of the rule of § 82, relating to the statute of limitations, and the two rules are similar in many respects. But only a few States have enacted statutes requiring the promises described in this Section to be in writing. In modern times discharge in bankruptcy has been thought to reflect a somewhat stronger public policy than the statute of limitations, and a promise implied from acknowledgement or part payment does not revive a debt discharged in bankruptcy. Although in the absence of a statute an oral promise is effective, the courts have insisted on the formality of express promise, denying effect to expressions of expectation or of good intention.

§ 84. Promise to Perform a Duty in Spite of Non-Occurrence of a Condition

(1) Except as stated in Subsection (2), a promise to perform all or part of a conditional duty under an antecedent contract in spite of the non-occurrence of the condition is binding, whether the promise is made before or after the time for the condition to occur, unless

(a) occurrence of the condition was a material part of the agreed exchange for the performance of the duty and the promisee was under no duty that it occur; or

(b) uncertainty of the occurrence of the condition was an element of the risk assumed by the promisor.

(2) If such a promise is made before the time for the occurrence of the condition has expired and the condition is within the control of the promisee or a beneficiary, the promisor can make his duty again subject to the condition by notifying the promisee or beneficiary of his intention to do so if

(a) the notification is received while there is still a reasonable time to cause the condition to occur under the antecedent terms or an extension given by the promisor; and

(b) reinstatement of the requirement of the condition is not unjust because of a material change of position by the promisee or beneficiary; and

(c) the promise is not binding apart from the rule stated in Subsection (1).

Comment:

a. Rationale. Like the rules stated in §§ 82 and 83, the rule of Subsection (1) can be thought of in terms of waiver of a defense not addressed to the merits, and rests in large part on the policies against forfeiture and unjust enrichment. Where the waiver is made before the time for the occurrence of the condition, it may induce nonoccurrence of the condition, and enforcement may also rest on reliance or on excuse by prevention or hindrance. See §§ 89, 90[.] But a waiver made after the original duty has been discharged, though it is sometimes said to "reinstate" the duty, in fact creates a new duty unqualified by the condition.

Conditions are the subject of more detailed treatment in §§ 224-29. In many situations an agreement or a rule of law, in the interest of simplicity and certainty, provides for absolute discharge of the promisor although a discharge to the extent of loss caused by a non-occurrence of condition might seem more equitable. . . . The likelihood of waiver and the pressure to find waiver or other excuse increases in proportion to the extent and unfairness of the forfeiture involved; in extreme cases the non-occurrence of the condition may be excused without other reason. See § 229.

Illustrations:

1. In an insurance policy the insurer promises to pay $1000 if the insured is killed on a railroad. The insurer's subsequent promise to pay $1000 even though the insured is not killed on a railroad is not binding under this Section, whether the promise is made before or after the death of the insured.

4. A, an insurance company, insures B's house for $5000 against loss by fire. The insurance policy provides that it shall be payable only if B gives written notification of any loss within thirty days after its occurrence. An insured loss occurs and B gives only oral notification thereof within thirty days. A tells him, either before or after the lapse of thirty days from the loss, that this notification is sufficient. A cannot thereafter rely upon B's failure to give written notification as an excuse for failure to pay for the loss.

6. In Illustration 4, A can restore the requirement of the condition by notifying B of his intention to do so if there still remains a reasonable time for the occurrence of the condition before the expiration of the thirty-day period, unless such action would be unjust in view of a material change of position by B in reliance on A's waiver. If a reasonable time does not remain, A cannot restore the requirement of the condition by extending the time.

§85. Promise to Perform a Voidable Duty

Except as stated in §93, a promise to perform all or part of an antecedent contract of the promisor, previously voidable by him, but not avoided prior to the making of the promise, is binding.

Comment:

a. Types of voidable contracts. The rule of this Section may be thought of as implicit in the definition of "voidable contract" in §7. Such a contract is distinguished from the "unenforceable contract" defined in §8 by the existence of a power of ratification. The power of avoidance may rest on lack of capacity under the rules stated in §§12-16, on mistake, misrepresentation, duress or undue influence under Chapters 6 and 7. In such cases exercise of the power of avoidance discharges the contractual duty and terminates the power of ratification; conversely, exercise of the power of ratification terminates the power of avoidance. . . .

b. Ratification and new promise. This Section relates only to action which constitutes a promise under the definition in § 2. Such a promise may be binding under this Section or because of its formal character or because it is supported by consideration or reliance. Even though it is "binding" under this Section, the new promise may itself be voidable for the same reason as the original promise, or it may be voidable or unenforceable for some other reason. See § 1, Comment *g*. In particular, a few states require the new promise of a former infant to be in writing and signed. A power of avoidance may also be lost in various other ways: by delay in giving notice, by failure to restore performance received, by exercise of dominion over things received, or by change of circumstances. See, e.g., as to avoidance for misrepresentation, § 164.

Illustration:

2. A, an infant, promises B to pay him $100 in consideration of a bicycle which B transfers to him. The bicycle is worth $60. On coming of age A promises to pay B the sum he originally agreed to pay. He is bound to do so. If instead of such a promise he promises to pay a smaller sum, as $40, he is also bound, but only to that extent.

§ 86. Promise for Benefit Received

(1) A promise made in recognition of a benefit previously received by the promisor from the promisee is binding to the extent necessary to prevent injustice.

(2) A promise is not binding under Subsection (1)

(a) if the promisee conferred the benefit as a gift or for other reasons the promisor has not been unjustly enriched; or

(b) to the extent that its value is disproportionate to the benefit.

Comment:

a. "Past consideration"; "moral obligation." Enforcement of promises to pay for benefit received has sometimes been said to rest on "past consideration" or on the "moral obligation" of the promisor, and there are statutes in such terms in a few states. Those terms are not used here: "past consideration" is inconsistent with the meaning of consideration stated in § 71, and there seems to be no consensus as to what constitutes a "moral obligation." The mere fact of promise has been thought to create a moral obligation, but it is clear that not all promises are enforced. Nor are moral obligations based solely on gratitude or sentiment sufficient of themselves to support a subsequent promise.

Illustration:

1. A gives emergency care to B's adult son while the son is sick and without funds far from home. B subsequently promises to reimburse A for his expenses. The promise is not binding under this Section.

b. Rationale. Although in general a person who has been unjustly enriched at the expense of another is required to make restitution, restitution is denied in many cases in order to protect persons who have had benefits thrust upon them. . . . In other cases restitution is denied by virtue of rules designed to guard against false claims, stale claims, claims already litigated, and the like. In many such cases a subsequent promise to make restitution removes the reason for the denial of relief, and the policy against unjust enrichment then prevails. . . . Enforcement of the subsequent promise sometimes makes it unnecessary to decide a difficult question as to the limits on quasi-contractual relief.

Many of the cases governed by the rules stated in §§ 82-85 are within the broader principle stated in this Section. But the broader principle is not so firmly established as those rules, and it may not be applied if there is doubt whether the objections to restitution are fully met by the subsequent promise. Facts such as the definite and substantial character of the benefit received, formality in the making of the promise, part performance of the promise, reliance on the promise or the probability of such reliance may be relevant to show that no imposition results from enforcement.

c. Promise to correct a mistake. One who makes a mistake in the conferring of a benefit is commonly entitled to restitution regardless of any promise. But restitution is often denied to avoid prejudice to the recipient of the benefit. Thus restitution of the value of services or of improvements to land or chattels may require a payment which the recipient cannot afford. . . . Where a subsequent promise shows that the usual protection is not needed in the particular case, restitution is granted to the extent promised.

Illustration:

4. A is employed by B to repair a vacant house. By mistake A repairs the house next door, which belongs to C. A subsequent promise by C to pay A the value of the repairs is binding.

d. Emergency services and necessaries. The law of restitution in the absence of promise severely limits recovery for necessaries furnished to a person under disability and for emergency services. . . . A subsequent promise in such a case may remove doubt as to the reality of the benefit and as to its value, and may negate any danger of imposition or false claim. A positive showing that payment was expected is not then required; an intention to make a gift must be shown to defeat restitution.

Illustration:

6. A finds B's escaped bull and feeds and cares for it. B's subsequent promise to pay reasonable compensation to A is binding.

i. Partial Enforcement. The rules stated in §§ 82-85 refer to promises to perform all or part of an antecedent duty, and do not make enforceable a promise to do more. Similarly, where a benefit received is a liquidated sum of money, a promise is not enforceable under this Section beyond the amount of the benefit. Where the value of the benefit is uncertain, a promise to pay the value is binding and a promise to pay a liquidated sum may serve to fix the amount due if in all the circumstances it is not disproportionate to the benefit. See Illustration 7. A promise which is excessive may sometimes be enforced to the extent of the value of the benefit, and the remedy may be thought of as quasi-contractual rather than contractual. In other cases a promise of disproportionate value may tend to show unfair pressure or other conduct by the promisee such that justice does not require any enforcement of the promise. Compare Comment *c* to § 72.

Illustrations:

12. A, a married woman of sixty, has rendered household services without compensation over a period of years for B, a man of eighty living alone and having no close relatives. B has a net worth of three million dollars and has

often assured A that she will be well paid for her services, whose reasonable value is not in excess of $6,000. B executes and delivers to A a written promise to pay A $25,000 "to be taken from my estate." The promise is binding.

13. The facts being otherwise as stated in Illustration 12, B's promise is made orally and is to leave A his entire estate. A cannot recover more than the reasonable value of her services.

§ 87. Option Contract

(1) An offer is binding as an option contract if it

(a) is in writing and signed by the offeror, recites a purported consideration for the making of the offer, and proposes an exchange on fair terms within a reasonable time; or

(b) is made irrevocable by statute.

(2) An offer which the offeror should reasonably expect to induce action or forbearance of a substantial character on the part of the offeree before acceptance and which does induce such action or forbearance is binding as an option contract to the extent necessary to avoid injustice.

Comment:

b. Nominal consideration. Offers made in consideration of one dollar paid or promised are often irrevocable under Subsection (1)(a). The irrevocability of an offer may be worth much or little to the offeree, and the courts do not ordinarily inquire into the adequacy of the consideration bargained for. See § 79. Hence a comparatively small payment may furnish consideration for the irrevocability of an offer proposing a transaction involving much larger sums. But gross disproportion between the payment and the value of the option commonly indicates that the payment was not in fact bargained for but was a mere formality or pretense. In such a case there is no consideration as that term is defined in § 71.

Nevertheless, such a nominal consideration is regularly held sufficient to support a short-time option proposing an exchange on fair terms. The fact that the option is an appropriate preliminary step in the conclusion of a socially useful transaction provides a sufficient substantive basis for enforcement, and a signed writing taking a form appropriate to a bargain satisfies the desiderata of form. In the absence of statute, however, the bargaining form is essential: a payment of one dollar by each party to the other is so obviously not a bargaining transaction that it does not provide even the form of an exchange.

Illustration:

1. In consideration of twenty-five cents paid by B, A executes and delivers to B a written option agreement giving B the right to buy a piece of land for $100,000 if B gives notice of intention to buy within 120 days. The price and terms of sale are fair. A has made an irrevocable offer.

c. False recital of nominal consideration. A recital in a written agreement that a stated consideration has been given is evidence of that fact as against a party to the agreement, but such a recital may ordinarily be contradicted by evidence that no such consideration was given or expected. See § 218. In cases within Subsection (1)(a), however, the giving and recital of nominal consideration performs a formal function only. The signed writing has vital significance as a formality, while the ceremonial manual delivery of a dollar or a peppercorn is an inconsequential formality. In view of the dangers of permitting a solemn written agreement to be invalidated by oral testimony which is easily fabricated, therefore, the option agreement is not invalidated by proof that the recited consideration was not in fact given. A fictitious rationalization has sometimes been used for this rule: acceptance of delivery of the written instrument conclusively imports a promise to make good the recital, it is said, and that promise furnishes consideration. Compare § 218. But the sound basis for the rule is that stated above.

Illustration:

3. A executes and delivers to B a written agreement "in consideration of one dollar in hand paid" giving B an option to buy described land belonging to A for $15,000, the option to expire at noon six days later. The fact that the dollar is not in fact paid does not prevent the offer from being irrevocable.

d. Statutory firm offers. In many states the seal is no longer an effective substitute for consideration[.] In addition, Uniform Commercial Code § 2-203 withdraws contracts and offers for the sale of goods from the law of sealed instruments. Statutes have sometimes given effect to a signed writing as a substitute formality, either generally or in cases of offers made in a signed writing and stated to be irrevocable. More common, however, are statutes dealing with particular types of offers. Thus when goods are put up at auction without reserve, an offer is made which is irrevocable under Uniform Commercial Code § 2-328(3). See § 28. Again, when statutes authorize or require that government work be awarded to contractors on the basis of competitive bidding, it may be fairly implied that the public officials in charge may protect the integrity of the competition by refusing to allow a bid to be withdrawn after the bids are opened. A similar implication may be drawn when an offer is required to be submitted to a court for approval. A more general provision for irrevocable offers is found in Uniform Commercial Code § 2-205, giving effect for a reasonable time not exceeding three months to a firm offer to buy or sell goods, made by a merchant in a signed writing.

§ 88. Guaranty

A promise to be surety for the performance of a contractual obligation, made to the obligee, is binding if

(a) the promise is in writing and signed by the promisor and recites a purported consideration; or

(b) the promise is made binding by statute; or

(c) the promisor should reasonably expect the promise to induce action or forbearance of a substantial character on the part of the promisee or a third person, and the promise does induce such action or forbearance.

§ 89. Modification of Executory Contract

A promise modifying a duty under a contract not fully performed on either side is binding

(a) if the modification is fair and equitable in view of circumstances not anticipated by the parties when the contract was made; or

(b) to the extent provided by statute; or

(c) to the extent that justice requires enforcement in view of material change of position in reliance on the promise.

Illustrations:

1. By a written contract A agrees to excavate a cellar for B for a stated price. Solid rock is unexpectedly encountered and A so notifies B. A and B then orally agree that A will remove the rock at a unit price which is reasonable but nine times that used in computing the original price, and A completes the job. B is bound to pay the increased amount.

3. A is employed by B as a designer of coats at $90 a week for a year beginning November 1 under a written contract executed September 1. A is offered $115 a week by another employer and so informs B. A and B then agree that A will be paid $100 a week and in October execute a new written contract to that effect, simultaneously tearing up the prior contract. The new contract is binding.

4. A contracts to manufacture and sell to B 2,000 steel roofs for corn cribs at $60. Before A begins manufacture a threat of a nationwide steel strike raises the cost of steel about $10 per roof. A thereafter manufactures and delivers 1,700 of the roofs, and B pays for 1,500 of them at the increased price without protest, increasing the selling price of the corn cribs by $10. The new agreement is binding.

§ 90. Promise Reasonably Inducing Action or Forbearance

(1) A promise which the promisor should reasonably expect to induce action or forbearance on the part of the promisee or a third person and which does induce such action or forbearance is binding if injustice can be avoided only by enforcement of the promise. The remedy granted for breach may be limited as justice requires.

(2) A charitable subscription or a marriage settlement is binding under Subsection (1) without proof that the promise induced action or forbearance.

Comment:

a. Relation to other rules. Obligations and remedies based on reliance are not peculiar to the law of contracts. This Section is often referred to in terms of "promissory estoppel," a phrase suggesting an extension of the doctrine of estoppel. Estoppel prevents a person from showing the truth contrary to a representation of fact made by him after another has relied on the representation. . . . Reliance is also a significant feature of numerous rules in the law of negligence, deceit and restitution. . . . In some cases those rules and this Section overlap; in others they provide analogies useful in determining the extent to which enforcement is necessary to avoid injustice.

It is fairly arguable that the enforcement of informal contracts in the action of assumpsit rested historically on justifiable reliance on a promise. Certainly reliance is one of the main bases for enforcement of the half-completed exchange, and the probability of reliance lends support to the enforcement of the executory exchange. See Comments to §§ 72, 75. This Section thus states a basic principle which often renders inquiry unnecessary as to the precise scope of the policy of enforcing bargains. Sections 87-89 state particular applications of the same principle to promises ancillary to bargains, and it also applies in a wide variety of non-commercial situations. . . .

Illustration:

1. A, knowing that B is going to college, promises B that A will give him $5,000 on completion of his course. B goes to college, and borrows and spends more than $5,000 for college expenses. When he has nearly completed his course, A notifies him of an intention to revoke the promise. A's promise is binding and B is entitled to payment on completion of the course without regard to whether his performance was "bargained for" under § 71.

b. Character of reliance protected. The principle of this Section is flexible. The promisor is affected only by reliance which he does or should foresee, and enforcement must be necessary to avoid injustice. Satisfaction of the latter requirement may depend on the reasonableness of the promisee's reliance, on its definite and substantial character in relation to the remedy sought, on the formality with which the promise is made, on the extent to which the evidentiary, cautionary, deterrent and channeling functions of form are met by the commercial setting or otherwise, and on the extent to which such other policies as the enforcement of bargains and the prevention of unjust enrichment are relevant. Compare Comment to § 72. The force of particular factors varies in different types of cases: thus reliance need not be of substantial character in charitable subscription cases, but must in cases of firm offers and guaranties. Compare Subsection (2) with §§ 87, 88.

d. Partial enforcement. A promise binding under this section is a contract, and full-scale enforcement by normal remedies is often appropriate. But the same factors which bear on whether any relief should be granted also bear on the character and extent of the remedy. In particular, relief may sometimes be limited to restitution or to damages or specific relief measured by the extent of the promisee's reliance rather than by the terms of the promise. See §§ 84, 89[.]

Unless there is unjust enrichment of the promisor, damages should not put the promisee in a better position than performance of the promise would have put him. See §§ 344, 349. In the case of a promise to make a gift it would rarely be proper to award consequential damages which would place the greater burden on the promisor than performance would have imposed.

§ 91. Effect of Promises Enumerated in §§ 82-90 When Conditional

If a promise within the terms of §§ 82-90 is in terms conditional or performable at a future time the promisor is bound thereby, but performance becomes due only upon the occurrence of the condition or upon the arrival of the specified time.

CHAPTER 5 THE STATUTE OF FRAUDS

Statutory Note: *The English statute.* The English Statute of Frauds, entitled "An Act for the Prevention of Frauds and Perjuries," 29 Charles II, c. 3, was enacted in 1677. Sections 4 and 17, dealing with contracts, were as follows:

> § 4. ". . . no action shall be brought whereby to charge any executor or administrator upon any special promise, to answer damages out of his own estate; (2) or whereby to charge the defendant upon any special promise to answer for the debt, default or miscarriages of another person; (3) or to charge any person upon any agreement made upon consideration of marriage; (4) or upon any contract or sale of lands, tenements or hereditaments, or any interest in or concerning them; (5) or upon any agreement that is not to be performed within the space of one year from the making thereof; (6) unless the agreement upon which such action shall be brought, or some memorandum or note thereof, shall be in writing, and signed by the party to be charged therewith, or some other person thereunto by him lawfully authorized.
>
> § 17. ". . . no contract for the sale of any goods, wares and merchandises, for the price of ten pounds sterling or upwards, shall be allowed to be good, except the buyer shall accept part of the goods so sold, and actually receive the same, or give something in earnest to bind the bargain, or in part of payment, or that some note or memorandum in writing of the said bargain be made and signed by the parties to be charged by such contract, or their agents thereunto lawfully authorized." . . .

American Statutes. Section 4 of the English statute was generally copied in the United States, and the American Statutes remain in force. In Maryland and New Mexico the English statute is in force by judicial decision. All the other states but Louisiana have statutes similar to the English statute, with some provisions omitted in a few states.

Other similar statutes. Many states deny enforcement to additional classes of contracts unless evidenced by a signed writing. Among the more common statutes are those requiring a writing for a contract to pay a commission to a real estate broker or business opportunity broker; for contracts to make a testamentary disposition or contracts not to be performed before the end of a lifetime; for promises to pay a debt contracted in infancy; and arbitration agreements. See Uniform Arbitration Act § 1. In addition, statutes regulating security agreements such as conditional sales and chattel mortgages have traditionally included a requirement of a writing; such statutes have been generally replaced by the Uniform Commercial Code. Statutes regulating retail installment sales also commonly impose formal requirements including a signed writing.

The Uniform Commercial Code. In the United States most statutes modeled on § 17 of the English Statute of Frauds were replaced by § 4 of the Uniform Sales Act, promulgated in 1906. More recently, the Sales Act has in turn been replaced by the Uniform Commercial Code. Sections 2-201, 8-319, 9-203 and 1-206 of the Code are reflected in § 178(2) and (3), but the Code provisions are not elaborated in this Restatement. Every state but Louisiana has now enacted the Uniform Commercial Code, and Louisiana has adopted Article 1.

The statutory purpose. As to the functions which legal formalities in general may serve, see Comment *c* to § 72. In general the primary purpose of the Statute of Frauds is assumed to be evidentiary, to provide reliable evidence of the existence and terms of the contract, and the classes of contracts covered seem for the most part to have been selected because of importance or complexity. Historical records provide no evidence that the draftsmen had a cautionary purpose, but the Statute serves such a purpose at least in the cases covered by the suretyship and marriage provisions. The land contract provision, together with formal requirements for the conveyance of land, performs a channeling function: it has helped to create a climate in which parties often regard their agreements as tentative until there is a signed writing. These additional functions have sometimes been reflected in judicial decisions and have played a part in discussion of the desirability of repeal.

§ 110. Classes of Contracts Covered

(1) The following classes of contracts are subject to a statute, commonly called the Statute of Frauds, forbidding enforcement unless there is a written memorandum or an applicable exception:

(a) a contract of an executor or administrator to answer for a duty of his decedent (the executor-administrator provision);

(b) a contract to answer for the duty of another (the suretyship provision);

(c) a contract made upon consideration of marriage (the marriage provision);

(d) a contract for the sale of an interest in land (the land contract provision);

(e) a contract that is not to be performed within one year from the making thereof (the one-year provision).

(2) The following classes of contracts, which were traditionally subject to the Statute of Frauds, are now governed by Statute of Frauds provisions of the Uniform Commercial Code:

(a) a contract for the sale of goods for the price of $500 or more (Uniform Commercial Code § 2-201);

(b) a contract for the sale of securities (Uniform Commercial Code § 8-319);

(c) a contract for the sale of personal property not otherwise covered, to the extent of enforcement by way of action or defense beyond $5,000 in amount or value of remedy (Uniform Commercial Code § 1-206).

(3) In addition the Uniform Commercial Code requires a writing signed by the debtor for an agreement which creates or provides for a security interest in personal property or fixtures not in the possession of the secured party.

(4) Statutes in most states provide that no acknowledgment or promise is sufficient evidence of a new or continuing contract to take a case out of the operation of a statute of limitations unless made in some writing signed by the party to be charged, but that the statute does not alter the effect of any payment of principal or interest.

(5) In many states other classes of contracts are subject to a requirement of a writing.

Comment:

a. Classes of contracts. The five different classes of contracts listed in Subsection (1) were included in different language in § 4 of the English Statute of Frauds, enacted in 1677. The English Statute was repealed in 1954 except for the suretyship and land contract provisions. Subsection (2) and (3) refer to four separate Statute of Frauds sections found in the Uniform Commercial Code, which displace § 4 of the Uniform Sales Act and § 17 of the English statute. The Code sections are not elaborated in this Restatement. Subsection (4) is a statement of a provision of Lord Tenterden's Act, 1828, which has been widely copied in the United States. As to the extent of enactment of these and other similar statutes, see the Statutory Note preceding this Section. The formal contracts referred to in § 6 of this Restatement are not affected by the Statute of Frauds, but in some cases are subject to separate statutes containing formal requirements.

b. Overlap of classes. The clauses of the English Statute apply separately; one contract may be within more than one clause of the statute, and facts which except it from one class may not except it from another. Thus contracts in consideration of marriage or for the sale of land or goods may also be contracts not to be performed within a year, and the statutory requirements in one clause may be satisfied and those of another clause unsatisfied.

Illustration:

1. A and B orally agree to marry three years later. The contract is unenforceable because not to be performed within a year, even though it is excepted from the provision for contracts in consideration of marriage.

c. Variations in the statutes. The English Statute of Frauds and many American statutes take the form, "No action shall be brought whereby to charge . . . unless. . . ." In some states non-complying contracts are said to be "void" or "invalid" or "not binding," but in spite of such differences there is much similarity in the interpretation given. Lord Tenterden's Act and Statutes modeled on it, however, are generally construed to require the acknowledgement or promise itself to be in writing; under such statutes a subsequent memorandum does not render enforceable a prior oral promise. See § 136.

d. Consequences of non-compliance. The consequences of non-compliance are the subject of Topic 7, §§ 138-[145]. In general a contract subject to the Statute of Frauds is unenforceable if the requirements of the statute are not satisfied. See § 8. The Statute does not in general bar the remedy of restitution; indeed, recovery of benefits conferred pursuant to an unenforceable contract is a standard remedy. See § 375[.] Where there has been part performance or other action in reliance on an unenforceable contract, the effect is in some situations to make the contract fully enforceable, in others to make particular remedies available. See, e.g., § 129. Even though no such rule is applicable, the circumstances may be such that justice requires enforcement of the promise. To the extent that justice so requires, the promise is then enforced by virtue of the doctrine of estoppel or by virtue of reliance on a promise notwithstanding the Statute. See § 139.

TOPIC 1. THE EXECUTOR-ADMINISTRATOR PROVISION

§ 111. Contract of Executor or Administrator

A contract of an executor or administrator to answer personally for a duty of his decedent is within the Statute of Frauds if a similar contract to answer for the duty of a living person would be within the Statute as a contract to answer for the duty of another.

Illustrations:

1. S, executor of D, promises C, a creditor of D at the time of D's death, in consideration of C's promise to forego part of the debt, to guarantee payment of the balance by the estate. S's promise is within the executor provision.

2. S, executor of D, contracts with C for funeral services, or for work and material necessary in closing D's business, promising orally "I guarantee that D's estate will pay you." S's promise is not within the executor provision.

Comment:

b. Exceptions. The executor provision is subject to the same exceptions as the suretyship provision. See Topic 2, §§ 112-23; Restatement of Security §§ 89-100. Thus the rule relating to novations stated in § 115 and the "main purpose" rule stated in § 116 are similarly applied to promises of executors or administrators.

TOPIC 2. THE SURETYSHIP PROVISION

§ 112. Requirement of Suretyship

A contract is not within the Statute of Frauds as a contract to answer for the duty of another unless the promisee is an obligee of the other's duty, the promisor is a surety for the other, and the promisee knows or has reason to know of the suretyship provision.

Comment:

a. The statutory purpose. In general the primary purpose of the Statute of Frauds is assumed to be evidentiary. See Statutory Note preceding § 110. In the case of suretyship contracts, however, the Statute also serves the cautionary function of guarding the promisor against ill-considered action. The suretyship provision is not limited to important or complex contracts, but is limited to suretyship and to promises made to an obligee of the principal obligation. Such promises serve a useful purpose, and the requirement of consideration is commonly met by the same promise or performance which is consideration for the principal obligation. See Comment to § 72; compare § 88. But the motivation of the surety is often essentially gratuitous, his obligation depends on a contingency which may seem remote at the time of contracting, and natural formalities which often attend an extension of credit are likely not to provide reliable evidence of the existence and terms of the surety's undertaking. Hence the requirement of a writing. Reliance of the kinds usual in suretyship situations—extension of credit or forbearance to pursue the principal obligor—does not render the requirement inapplicable.

Illustration:

1. D commits a tort against C. S promises C orally for consideration to pay C the damages which C has suffered from the tort if D fails to do so. S's promise is within the Statute of Frauds, since D is under a direct duty to C, and S's promise is to perform D's duty if D fails to do so.

c. Promisor must be surety. The suretyship provision applied only if there is a principal obligation "of another" than the promisor. The promisor must promise as a surety for the principal obligor. Whether the promisor and the other are surety and principal depends on their contract or relation to each other. The essential elements of the relation are that they are bound for the same performance and that as between them the other rather than the promisor should perform. See Restatement of Security §82. A promise to be surety for part of the principal obligation is within the Statute, but a promise of a distinct performance is not, even though its purpose is to render more certain the performance of the principal obligation.

Illustration:

6. In consideration of the delivery of goods by C to D at S's request, S orally promises to pay the price of them. S's promise is not within the Statute of Frauds, since D is under no duty.

§113. Promises of the Same Performance for the Same Consideration

Where promises of the same performance are made by two persons for a consideration which inures to the benefit of only one of them, the promise of the other is within the Statute of Frauds as a contract to answer for the duty of another, whether or not the promise is in terms conditional on default by the one to whose benefit the consideration inures, unless

(a) the other is not a surety for the one to whose benefit the consideration inures; or

(b) the promises are in terms joint and do not create several duties or joint and several duties; or

(c) the promisee neither knows nor has reason to know that the consideration does not inure to the benefit of both promisors.

§114. Independent Duty of Promisor

A, contract to perform or otherwise to satisfy all or part of a duty of a third person to the promisee is not within the Statute of Frauds as a contract to answer for the duty of another if, by the terms of the promise when it is made, performance thereof can involve no more than

(a) the application of funds or property held by the promisor for the purpose, or

(b) performance of any other duty owing, irrespective of his promise, by the promisor to the promisee, or

(c) performance of a duty which is either owing, irrespective of his promise, by the promisor to the third person, or which the promisee reasonably believes to be so owing.

§ 115. Novation

A contract that is itself accepted in satisfaction of a previously existing duty of a third person to the promisee is not within the Statute of Frauds as a contract to answer for the duty of another.

§ 116. Main Purpose: Advantage to Surety

A contract that all or part of a duty of a third person to the promisee shall be satisfied is not within the Statute of Frauds as a promise to answer for the duty of another if the consideration for the promise is in fact or apparently desired by the promisor mainly for his own economic advantage, rather than in order to benefit the third person. If, however, the consideration is merely a premium for insurance, the contract is within the Statute.

Comment:

a. Rationale. This Section states what is often called the "main purpose" or "leading object" rule. Where the surety-promisor's main purpose is his own pecuniary or business advantage, the gratuitous or sentimental element often present in suretyship is eliminated, the likelihood of disproportion in the values exchanged between promisor and promisee is reduced, and the commercial context commonly provides evidentiary safeguards. Thus there is less need for cautionary or evidentiary formality than in other cases of suretyship. The situation is comparable to a sale or purchase of a third person's obligation, which is also outside the purposes of the suretyship provision of the Statute of Frauds. See §§ 121, 122. Historically, the rule could be reconciled with the words of the Statute on the ground that a promisor who received a bargained-for benefit could be sued in debt of *indebitatus assumpsit*; hence he promised to pay his own debt rather than the debt "of another," and the promise was not "special" in the sense that special assumpsit was the only appropriate remedy. In modern times, however, the rule is applied in terms of its reason rather than to accord with abandoned procedural categories.

Illustrations:

1. D owes C $1,000. C is about to levy an attachment on D's factory. S, who is a friend of D's desiring to prevent his friend's financial ruin, orally promises C that if C will forbear to take legal proceedings against D for three months, S will pay D's debt if D fails to do so. S had no purpose to benefit himself and C has no reason to suppose so. S's promise is not enforceable.

2. D owes C $1,000. C is about to levy an attachment on D's factory. S, who is also a creditor of D's, fearing that the attachment will ruin D's business and thereby destroy his own chance of collecting his claim, orally promises C that if C will forbear to take legal proceedings against D for three months, S will pay D's debt if D fails to do so. S's promise is enforceable.

TOPIC 3. THE MARRIAGE PROVISION

§124. Contract Made Upon Consideration of Marriage

A promise for which all or part of the consideration is either marriage or a promise to marry is within the Statute of Frauds, except in the case of an agreement which consists only of mutual promises of two persons to marry each other.

Comment:

a. Engagement to marry. Mutual promises to marry were within the words of the English statute, but were not within the statutory purpose and were soon excluded by judicial interpretation. A number of American statutes explicitly except such promises from the marriage provision. They may, however, fall within the one-year provision. Statutes in many states bar actions for breach of a promise to marry.

b. Marriage settlements. A promise to transfer property to a husband or wife or to a third person or a promise regulating the property interests of husband and wife is within the Statute of Frauds if the consideration includes marriage or a promise to marry, whether or not mutual promises to marry are part of the agreement. Such a promise may be made by one of the parties to the contemplated marriage or by a third person.

Illustrations:

1. In consideration of A's promise to marry B, B orally promises to marry A and to settle Blackacre upon A. B's promise is within the Statute of Frauds.
2. B offers to marry A. To induce A to accept the offer, B orally promises to settle property upon A. A accepts the offer. Both promises to marry and B's promise to make a settlement are within the Statute of Frauds.
3. In consideration of A's promise to marry B, B orally promises to marry A and to forego the rights which the law allows B with reference to A's property. B's promise is within the Statute of Frauds.
4. In consideration of A's marrying B, C orally promises A a settlement. C's promise is within the Statute of Frauds.

c. Promise in contemplation of marriage. A promise is not within the Statute merely because it is conditional on marriage, or because marriage is contemplated by the promisor or the promisee or both. The marriage or promise to marry must be bargained for and given in exchange for the promise. See §71.

Illustrations:

5. A and B mutually promise that each will settle $5,000 on A's daughter when she marries B's son. The promises are not within the Statute of Frauds, since the marriage is a condition rather than consideration.
6. A and B are engaged to marry. In consideration of A's promise that when married they will live in a house owned by A, B promises to settle $10,000 upon her. The promises are not within the marriage provision of the Statute of Frauds.

TOPIC 4. THE LAND CONTRACT PROVISION

§ 125. Contract to Transfer, Buy, or Pay for an Interest in Land

(1) A promise to transfer to any person any interest in land is within the Statute of Frauds.

(2) A promise to buy any interest in land is within the Statute of Frauds, irrespective of the person to whom the transfer is to be made.

(3) When a transfer of an interest in land has been made, a promise to pay the price, if originally within the Statute of Frauds, ceases to be within it unless the promised price is itself in whole or in part an interest in land.

(4) Statutes in most states except from the land contract and one-year provisions of the Statute of Frauds short-term leases and contracts to lease, usually for a term not longer than one year.

Comment:

c. Contract to sell. The land contract provision applies to any executory promise to transfer an interest in land, whether the consideration is money, chattels, services, other land, or something else, and whether the land is to be transferred to the promisee or to someone else. "Transfer" for this purpose includes the creation or extinguishing of an interest with the effect of giving another an interest he did not previously have, and "promise to transfer" includes an option contract. But the provision does not apply to a promise to refrain from making a transfer, or to a promise to divide profits if land is sold. In some cases, despite a failure to satisfy the Statute, a resulting or constructive trust is imposed on one who has acquired land or other property under the contract. . . .

Illustrations:

5. For consideration, A promises B to devise Blackacre to B. A's promise is within the Statute.

7. A orally promises B to share with him whatever proceeds A obtains from the sale of Blackacre. A's promise is not within the land contract provision of the Statute of Frauds.

d. Contract to buy. The land contract provision applies to a contract to buy as well as to a contract to sell. It covers a promise to pay for a conveyance of an interest in land, so long as the conveyance has not been made, whether the price is to be paid in money, in goods, services or other land, or otherwise, and whether the conveyance is to be made to the promisor or to a third person. But the Statute does not prevent enforcement of a negotiable instrument given in part payment under an oral land contract.

Illustration:

9. A promises to support B during B's life in consideration of B's promise to convey Blackacre to A. A's promise is within the Statute of Frauds.

e. Effect of conveyance. Payment of the price for land does not of itself take a land contract out of the Statute of Frauds. See § 129. But once the transfer has been made, the promise to pay the price becomes enforceable, unless the price is land. Compare § 147.

Illustration:

11. A promises B to transfer Blackacre to B, in consideration of B's promise to pay A $5,000. A tenders a deed of Blackacre to B and B accepts the deed. B's promise is no longer within the land contract provision of the Statute of Frauds.

§ 127. Interest in Land

An interest in land within the meaning of the Statute is any right, privilege, power or immunity, or combination thereof, which is an interest in land under the law of property and is not "goods" within the Uniform Commercial Code.

Comment:

a. Property interests. In applying the land contract provision of the Statute of Frauds, the test of what is an interest in land is in general that furnished by the law of property. . . . Leaseholds are included unless within an exception for short-term leases. Both present and future interests, legal and equitable, are interests in land for this purpose, including the interests of mortgagor and mortgagee or of vendor and purchaser under a specifically enforceable contract.

§ 129. Action in Reliance; Specific Performance

A contract for the transfer of an interest in land may be specifically enforced notwithstanding failure to comply with the Statute of Frauds if it is established that the party seeking enforcement, in reasonable reliance on the contract and on the continuing assent of the party against whom enforcement is sought, has so changed his position that injustice can be avoided only by specific enforcement.

TOPIC 5. THE ONE-YEAR PROVISION

§ 130. Contract Not to Be Performed Within a Year

(1) Where any promise in a contract cannot be fully performed within a year from the time the contract is made, all promises in the contract are within

the Statute of Frauds until one party to the contract completes his performance.

(2) When one party to a contract has completed his performance, the one-year provision of the Statute does not prevent enforcement of the promises of other parties.

Comment:

a. Possibility of performance within one year. The English Statute of Frauds applied to an action "upon any agreement that is not to be performed within the space of one year from the making thereof." The design was said to be not to trust to the memory of witnesses for a longer time than one year, but the statutory language was not appropriate to carry out that purpose. The result has been a tendency to construction narrowing the application of the statute. Under the prevailing interpretation, the enforceability of a contract under the one-year provision does not turn on the actual course of subsequent events, nor on the expectations of the parties as to the probabilities. Contracts of uncertain duration are simply excluded; the provision covers only those contracts whose performance cannot possibly be completed within a year.

Illustrations:

1. A, an insurance company, orally promises to insure B's house against fire for five years, B promising to pay the premium therefor within the week. The contract is not within the Statute of Frauds, since if the house burns and the insurer pays within a year the contract will be fully performed.

2. A orally promises to work for B, and B promises to employ A during A's life at a stated salary. The promises are not within the one-year provision of the Statute, since A's life may terminate within a year.

3. A and B, a railway, agree that A will provide grading and ties and B will construct a switch and maintain it as long as A needs it for shipping purposes. A plans to use it for shipping lumber from adjoining land which contains enough lumber to run a mill for 30 years, and uses the switch for 15 years. The contract is not within the one-year provision of the Statute.

4. A orally promises B to sell him five crops of potatoes to be grown on a specified farm in Minnesota, and B promises to pay a stated price on delivery. The contract is within the Statute of Frauds. It is impossible in Minnesota for five crops of potatoes to mature in one year.

b. Discharge within a year. Any contract may be discharged by a subsequent agreement of the parties, and performance of many contracts may be excused by supervening events or by the exercise of a power to cancel granted by the contract. The possibility that such a discharge or excuse may occur within a year is not a possibility that the contract will be "performed" within a year. This is so even though the excuse is articulated in the agreement. This distinction between performance and excuse for nonperformance is sometimes tenuous; it depends on the terms and the circumstances, particularly on whether the essential purposes of the parties will be attained. Discharge by death of the promisor may be the equivalent of performance in the case of a promise to forbear, such as a contract not to compete.

Illustrations:

5. A orally promises to work for B, and B promises to employ A for five years at a stated salary. The promises are within the Statute of Frauds. Though the duties of both parties will be discharged if A dies within a year, the duties cannot be "performed" within a year. This conclusion is not affected by a term in the oral agreement that the employment shall terminate on A's death.

6. The facts being otherwise as stated in Illustration 5, the agreement provides that either party may terminate the contract by giving 30 days notice at any time. The agreement is one of uncertain duration and is not within the one-year provision of the Statute.

7. The facts being otherwise as stated in Illustration 5, the agreement provides that A may quit at any time. The agreement is within the Statute.

8. A, the maternal grandmother of a new-born illegitimate child, agrees with B, the father, that A will care for the child and B will make support payments until the child becomes 21 years old. The agreement is not within the one-year provision of the Statute. If the child dies within a year, the primary object of furnishing necessaries to the child will be fully "performed."

9. A sells his grocery business to B, who pays part of the price and promises to pay the balance in a month, A agreeing orally not to engage in the grocery business in the same town for five years. The contract is not within the one-year provision of the Statute, since A's death within one year will give B the equivalent of full performance.

d. Full performance on one side. If either party promises a performance that cannot be completed within a year, the Statute applies to all promises in the contract, including those which can or even must be performed within a year. But unlike other provisions of the Statute, the one-year provision does not apply to a contract which is performed on one side at the time it is made, such as a loan of money, nor to any contract which has been fully performed on one side, whether the performance is completed within a year or not. This rule, by permitting an action for the agreed price, avoids the problem of valuation which would otherwise arise in an action for the value of benefits conferred; but the rule goes further and makes available the usual contract remedies.

Illustration:

14. A promises to pay B $5,000 in two years in return for B's promise to render a stated performance for five years. A pays the $5,000 as agreed. B then refuses further performance. The contract is withdrawn from the operation of the Statute.

e. Part performance. Part performance not amounting to full performance on one side does not in general take a contract out of the one-year provision. Restitution is available in such cases, and doctrines of estoppels and fraud may be applicable. See §§ 139, 375. Where the contract provides the price or rate to be paid for the part performance, the performing party will normally recover according to the contract; in other cases, the contract terms are evidence of reasonable value.

Illustration:

15. A and B contract orally for A's employment by B at a stated salary for the ensuing two years. A works under the contract for 15 months when B discharges him without cause. The contract is not withdrawn from the operation of the Statute, and A may not recover damages for wrongful discharge. But A may recover any unpaid salary.

TOPIC 6. SATISFACTION OF THE STATUTE BY A MEMORANDUM

§ 131. General Requisites of a Memorandum

Unless additional requirements are prescribed by the particular statute, a contract within the Statute of Frauds is enforceable if it is evidenced by any writing, signed by or on behalf of the party to be charged, which

(a) reasonably identifies the subject matter of the contract,

(b) is sufficient to indicate that a contract with respect thereto has been made between the parties or offered by the signer to the other party, and

(c) states with reasonable certainty the essential terms of the unperformed promises in the contract.

Comment:

c. Rationale. The primary purpose of the Statute is evidentiary, to require reliable evidence of the existence and terms of the contract and to prevent enforcement through fraud or perjury of contracts never in fact made. The contents of the writing must be such as to make successful fraud unlikely, but the possibility need not be excluded that some other subject matter or person than those intended will also fall within the words of the writing. Where only an evidentiary purpose is served, the requirement of a memorandum is read in the light of the dispute which arises and the admissions of the party to be charged; there is no need for evidence on points not in dispute.

The suretyship and marriage provisions of the Statute perform a cautionary as well as an evidentiary function. See §§ 112, 124. The land contract provision performs a channeling function. See Statutory Note preceding § 110. Even where these provisions are involved, however, there is no evidence of a statutory purpose to facilitate repudiation of firm oral agreements fairly made, to protect a promisor from temptation to perjure himself by false denial of the promise, or to reward a candid contract-breaker by denying enforcement.

d. Types of documents. The statutory memorandum may be a written contract, but under the traditional statutory language any writing, formal or informal, may be sufficient, including a will, a notation on a check, a receipt, a pleading, or an informal letter. Neither delivery nor communication is essential. See § 133.

Writing for this purpose includes any intentional reduction to tangible form. See Uniform Commercial Code § 1-201.

Illustrations:

1. A makes an oral contract with B to devise Blackacre to B, and executes a will containing the devise and a recital of the contract. The will is revoked by a later will. The revoked will is a sufficient memorandum to charge A's estate.

2. A publishes in a newspaper an offer to buy certain goods, stating the terms of his proposal, and his name is printed under the advertisement. B accepts the offer. The advertisement is a sufficient memorandum to charge A. See § 136.

3. A writes and signs in pencil a receipt for $1,000 which recites that the money is received from B as part payment of the price of $5,000 for a parcel of land. The receipt is a sufficient memorandum to charge A on the agreement recited.

e. Subject matter. A memorandum, like a contract, must be read in its context and need not be comprehensible to persons not familiar with the particular type of transaction. Without reference to executor oral promises, the memorandum in context must indicate with reasonable certainty the nature of the transaction and must provide a basis for identifying the land, goods or other subject matter.

Illustrations:

4. A company executes a written contract with B by which B purchases certain accounts owned by A Company. As part of the same transaction, C, the president of A Company, signs a contract of guaranty printed at the foot of the same paper: "In order to induce B to enter into an agreement dated _____ with _____ (Hereinafter referred to as the client), the undersigned agrees to be liable for due performance of all the client's agreements with B." The blanks are not filled in. The quoted words are sufficient to identify the obligation guaranteed.

7. A and B enter into a contract by which A promises to sell and B to buy a certain lot of hops belonging to A. A telegram from B refers to the subject matter as "number 13." This refers to a sample submitted by A to B by mail with a numbered tag attached and referring by trade usage to a specific lot. The description is sufficient.

f. Contract between the parties. A memorandum must be sufficient to indicate that a contract has been made between the parties with respect to an identified subject matter or that the signer has offered such a contract to the other party. The parties must be reasonably identified; the identification may consist of a name or initials, even though there may be others with the same name or initials, or of any other reasonably accurate mode of description. Identification of the agent of a party in the memorandum sufficiently refers to the party, whether or not the agent is himself a party. . . . Where there is no dispute as to the parties, a party may be sufficiently identified by possession of a memorandum signed by the other party. A signed written offer to the public may be sufficient even though the offeree is not identified.

Illustration:

10. A and B are negotiating for the sale of A's restaurant to B. B gives A a check for $500 bearing the notation "tentative deposit on tentative purchase of 1415 City Line Ave., Phila. Restaurant, Fixtures, Equipment, Good Will." Later A and B orally agree on terms of sale. The quoted memorandum is not sufficient to indicate that a contract for sale has been made.

§ 132. Several Writings

The memorandum may consist of several writings if one of the writings is signed and the writings in the circumstances clearly indicate that they relate to the same transaction.

§ 133. Memorandum Not Made as Such

Except in the case of a writing evidencing a contract upon consideration of marriage, the Statute may be satisfied by a signed writing not made as a memorandum of a contract.

§ 134. Signature

The signature to a memorandum may be any symbol made or adopted with an intention, actual or apparent, to authenticate the writing as that of the signer.

§ 135. Who Must Sign

Where a memorandum of a contract within the Statute is signed by fewer than all parties to the contract and the Statute is not otherwise satisfied, the contract is enforceable against the signers but not against the others.

§ 136. Time of Memorandum

A memorandum sufficient to satisfy the Statute may be made or signed at any time before or after the formation of the contract.

§137. Loss or Destruction of a Memorandum

The loss or destruction of a memorandum does not deprive it of effect under the Statute.

Comment:

a. Not a rule of evidence. Although the Statute of Frauds was designed to serve an evidentiary purpose, it is not a rule of evidence. In cases of loss or destruction, the contents of a memorandum may be shown by an unsigned copy or by oral evidence. . . .

TOPIC 7. CONSEQUENCES OF NON-COMPLIANCE

§138. Unenforceability

Where a contract within the Statute of Frauds is not enforceable against the party to be charged by an action against him, it is not enforceable by a set-off or counterclaim in an action brought by him, or as a defense to a claim by him.

§139. Enforcement by Virtue of Action in Reliance

(1) A promise which the promisor should reasonably expect to induce action or forbearance on the part of the promisee or a third person and which does induce the action or forbearance is enforceable notwithstanding the Statute of Frauds if injustice can be avoided only by enforcement of the promise. The remedy granted for breach is to be limited as justice requires.

(2) In determining whether injustice can be avoided only by enforcement of the promise, the following circumstances are significant:

(a) the availability and adequacy of other remedies, particularly cancellation and restitution;

(b) the definite and substantial character of the action or forbearance in relation to the remedy sought;

(c) the extent to which the action or forbearance corroborates evidence of the making and terms of the promise, or the making and terms are otherwise established by clear and convincing evidence;

(d) the reasonableness of the action or forbearance;

(e) the extent to which the action or forbearance was foreseeable by the promisor.

Comment:

b. Avoidance of injustice. Like §90 this Section states a flexible principle, but the requirement of consideration is more easily displaced than the requirement of a writing. The reliance must be foreseeable by the promisor, and enforcement must be necessary to avoid injustice. Subsection (2) lists some of the relevant factors in applying the latter requirement. Each factor relates either to the extent to which reliance furnishes a compelling substantive basis for relief in addition to the expectations created by the promise or to the extent to which the circumstances satisfy the evidentiary purpose of the Statute and fulfill any cautionary, deterrent and channeling functions it may serve.

Illustration:

1. A is lessee of a building for five years at $75 per month and has sublet it for three years at $100 per month. A seeks to induce B to purchase the building, and to that end orally promises to assign to B the lease and sublease and to execute a written assignment as soon as B obtains a deed. B purchases the building in reliance on the promise. B is entitled to the rentals from the sublease.

§ 143. Unenforceable Contract as Evidence

The Statute of Frauds does not make an unenforceable contract inadmissible in evidence for any purpose other than its enforcement in violation of the Statute.

Illustration:

1. A renders services to B under an oral contract within the Statute by which B promises to pay for the services. On B's refusal to pay, A sues for the value of the services. The oral contract is admissible as evidence that the services were not rendered officiously or as a gift, and as evidence of the value of the services.

§ 144. Effect of Unenforceable Contract as to Third Parties

Only a party to a contract or a transferee or successor of a party to the contract can assert that the contract is unenforceable under the Statute of Frauds.

§ 145. Effect of Full Performance

Where the promises in a contract have been fully performed by all parties, the Statute of Frauds does not affect the legal relations of the parties.

CHAPTER 6 MISTAKE

§151. Mistake Defined

A mistake is a belief that is not in accord with the facts.

Comment:

b. Facts include law. The rules stated in this Chapter do not draw the distinction that is sometimes made between "fact" and "law." They treat the law in existence at the time of the making of the contract as part of the total state of facts at that time. A party's erroneous belief with respect to the law, as found in statute, regulation, judicial decision, or elsewhere, or with respect to the legal consequences of his acts, may, therefore, come within these rules.

§152. When Mistake of Both Parties Makes a Contract Voidable

(1) Where a mistake of both parties at the time a contract was made as to a basic assumption on which the contract was made has a material effect on the agreed exchange of performances, the contract is voidable by the adversely affected party unless he bears the risk of the mistake under the rule stated in §154.

(2) In determining whether the mistake has a material effect on the agreed exchange of performances, account is taken of any relief by way of reformation, restitution, or otherwise.

Comment:

b. Basic assumption. A mistake of both parties does not make the contract voidable unless it is one as to the basic assumption on which both parties made the contract. The term "basic assumption" has the same meaning here as it does in Chapter 11 in connection with impracticability (§§261, 266(1)) and frustration (§§265, 266(2)). See Uniform Commercial Code §2-615(a). For example, market conditions and the financial situation of the parties are ordinarily not such assumptions, and, generally, just as shifts in market conditions or financial ability do not effect discharge under the rules governing impracticability, mistakes as to market conditions or financial ability do not justify avoidance under the rules governing mistake. See Comment *b* to §261. The parties may have had such a "basic assumption," even though they were not conscious of alternatives. See Introductory Note to Chapter 11. Where, for example, a party purchases an annuity on the life of another person, it can be said that it was a basic assumption that the other person was alive at the time, even though the parties never consciously addressed themselves to the possibility that he was dead.

Illustration:

1. A contracts to sell and B to buy a tract of land, the value of which has depended mainly on the timber on it. Both A and B believe that the timber is still there, but in fact it has been destroyed by fire. The contract is voidable by B.

c. Material effect on agreed exchange. A party cannot avoid a contract merely because both parties were mistaken as to a basic assumption on which it was made. He must, in addition, show that the mistake has a material effect on the agreed exchange of performances. It is not enough for him to prove that he would not have made the contract had it not been for the mistake. He must show that the resulting imbalance in the agreed exchange is so severe that he cannot fairly be required to carry it out. Ordinarily he will be able to do this by showing that the exchange is not only less desirable to him but is also more advantageous to the other party. Sometimes this is so because the adversely affected party will give, and the other party will receive, something more than they supposed. Sometimes it is so because the other party will give, and the adversely affected party will receive, something less than they supposed. In such cases the materiality of the effect on the agreed exchange will be determined by the overall impact on both parties. In exceptional cases the adversely affected party may be able to show that the effect on the agreed exchange has been material simply on the ground that the exchange has become less desirable for him, even though there has been no effect on the other party. Cases of hardship that result in no advantage to the other party are, however, ordinarily appropriately left to the rules on impracticability and frustration. . . . The standard of materiality here, as elsewhere in this Restatement (e.g., § 237), is a flexible one to be applied in the light of all the circumstances.

Illustration:

8. A contracts to sell and B to buy a tract of land, which they believe contains 100 acres, at a price of $1,000 per acre. In fact the tract contains 110 acres. The contract is not voidable by either A or B, unless additional facts show that the effect on the agreed exchange of performances is material.

e. Allocation of risk. A party may be considered to have undertaken to perform in spite of a mistake that has a material effect on the agreed exchange of performances. He then bears the risk of the mistake. Because of the significance of the allocation of risk in the law of mistake, the scope of this exception is spelled out in detail in § 154 (It is assumed in the illustrations to the present Section that the adversely affected party does not bear the risk of the mistake under the rule stated in § 154. . . .

§ 153. When Mistake of One Party Makes a Contract Voidable

Where a mistake of one party at the time a contract was made as to a basic assumption on which he made the contract has a material effect on the agreed exchange of performances that is adverse to him, the contract is voidable by him if he does not bear the risk of the mistake under the rule stated in § 154, and

(a) the effect of the mistake is such that enforcement of the contract would be unconscionable, or

(b) the other party had reason to know of the mistake or his fault caused the mistake.

§ 154. When a Party Bears the Risk of a Mistake

A party bears the risk of a mistake when

(a) the risk is allocated to him by agreement of the parties, or

(b) he is aware, at the time the contract is made, that he has only limited knowledge with respect to the facts to which the mistake relates but treats his limited knowledge as sufficient, or

(c) the risk is allocated to him by the court on the ground that it is reasonable in the circumstances to do so.

§ 155. When Mistake of Both Parties as to Written Expression Justifies Reformation

Where a writing that evidences or embodies an agreement in whole or in part fails to express the agreement because of a mistake of both parties as to the contents or effect of the writing, the court may at the request of a party reform the writing to express the agreement, except to the extent that rights of third parties such as good faith purchasers for value will be unfairly affected.

Comment:

a. Scope. The province of reformation is to make a writing express the agreement that the parties intended it should. Under the rule stated in this Section, reformation is available when the parties, having reached an agreement and having then attempted to reduce it to writing, fail to express it correctly in the writing. Their mistake is one as to expression—one that relates to the contents or effect of the writing that is intended to express their agreement—and the appropriate remedy is reformation of that writing properly to reflect their agreement. For the rule stated in this Section to be invoked, therefore, there must have been some agreement between the parties prior to the writing. The prior agreement need not, however, be complete and certain enough to be a contract. Compare § 1 with § 3; see § 33. If the parties reach agreement as to only part of a prospective bargain, and if they are later mistaken in their attempt to put in writing this agreement together with such other terms as will make a contract, reformation is still an appropriate remedy. The agreement must, of course, be certain enough to permit a court to frame relief in terms of reformation. The writing that is reformed may purport to embody their entire agreement (i.e., a completely integrated agreement under § 210(1)), or only part of their agreement (i.e., a partially integrated agreement under § 210(2)), since the parol evidence rule does not preclude such a showing of mistake. See § 214(d). It may be a writing evidencing a contract within the Statute of Frauds, since the Statute does not bar reformation. See § 156. (If neither the parol evidence rule nor the Statute of Frauds applies, the writing itself will not ordinarily have sufficient legal significance for its reformation to be necessary.) The error in expressing the agreement may consist in the omission or erroneous reduction to writing of a term agreed upon or the inclusion of a term not agreed upon. If the parties are mistaken with respect to the legal effect of the language that they have used, the writing may be reformed to reflect the intended effect. Reformation is available even though the effect of the error is to make it appear from the writing that there is no enforceable agreement. See Illustration 2 and Comment a and Illustration 3 to § 156. Reformation is not precluded by the mere fact that the party who seeks it failed to exercise reasonable care in reading the writing, but the right to reformation is subject to the rule on fault stated in § 157. With the merger of law and equity under modern codes of procedure, it is generally unnecessary to seek reformation as a condition to enforcing the true contract, and a party may be granted both reformation and enforcement in a single suit.

§ 156. Mistake as to Contract Within the Statute of Frauds

If reformation of a writing is otherwise appropriate, it is not precluded by the fact that the Contract is within the statute of frauds.

§ 157. Effect of Fault of Party Seeking Relief

A mistaken party's fault in failing to know or discover the facts before making the contract does not bar him from avoidance or reformation under the rules stated in this Chapter, unless his fault amounts to a failure to act in good faith and in accordance with reasonable standards of fair dealing.

CHAPTER 7 MISREPRESENTATION, DURESS AND UNDUE INFLUENCE

TOPIC 1. MISREPRESENTATION

§ 159. Misrepresentation Defined

A misrepresentation is an assertion that is not in accord with the facts.

Comment:

a. Nature of the assertion. A misrepresentation, being a false assertion of fact, commonly takes the form of spoken or written words. Whether a statement is false depends on the meaning of the words in all the circumstances, including what may fairly be inferred from them. An assertion may also be inferred from conduct other than words. Concealment or even non-disclosure may have the effect of a misrepresentation under the rules stated in §§ 160 and 161. Whether a misrepresentation is fraudulent is determined by the rule stated in § 162(1). However, an assertion need not be fraudulent to be a misrepresentation. Thus a statement intended to be truthful may be a misrepresentation because of ignorance or carelessness, as when the word "not" is inadvertently omitted or when inaccurate language is used. But a misrepresentation that is not fraudulent has no consequences under this Chapter unless it is material. Whether an assertion is material is determined by the rule stated in § 162(2). The consequences of a misrepresentation are dealt with in §§ 163, 164 and 166.

Illustrations:

1. A, seeking to induce B to make a contract to buy a used car, turns the odometer back from 60,000 to 18,000 miles. B makes the contract. A's conduct in setting the odometer is a misrepresentation. Whether the contract is voidable by B is determined by the rule stated in § 164.

2. A, seeking to induce B to make a contract to lease a particular generator, writes B a letter with the intention of describing its output correctly as "1200 kilowatts." Because of an error of A's typist, unnoticed by A, the letter states that the output of the generator is 2100 kilowatts." B makes the contract. A's statement is a misrepresentation. Whether the contract is voidable by B is determined by the rule stated in § 164.

b. Half-truths. A statement may be true with respect to the facts stated, but may fail to include qualifying matter necessary to prevent the implication of an assertion that is false with respect to other facts. For example, a true statement that an event has recently occurred may carry the false implication that the situation has not changed since its occurrence. Such a half-truth may be as misleading as an assertion that is wholly false.

c. Meaning of "fact." An assertion must relate to something that is a fact at the time the assertion is made in order to be a misrepresentation. Such facts include past events as well as present circumstances but do not include future events. An assertion limited to future events (see § 2), may be a basis of liability for breach of contract, but not of relief for misrepresentation. However, a promise or a prediction of future events may by implication involve an assertion that facts exist from which the promised or predicted consequences will follow, which may be a misrepresentation as to those facts. Thus, from a statement that a particular machine will attain a specified level of performance when it is used, it may be inferred that its present design and condition make it capable of such a level. Such an inference may be drawn even if the statement is not legally binding as a promise.

Illustration:

5. A, seeking to induce B to make a contract to buy land, promises B to build an expensive house on an adjoining tract. A knows that he neither owns nor has such an interest in the tract that he can perform the promise, although he hopes to perform it. B makes the contract. A's promise implies an assertion that he owns the tract or has such an interest in the adjoining tract that he can perform his promise, and this assertion is a misrepresentation. Whether the contract is voidable by B is determined by the rule stated in § 164.

§ 160. When Action Is Equivalent to an Assertion (Concealment)

Action intended or known to be likely to prevent another from learning a fact is equivalent to an assertion that the fact does not exist.

Comment:

b. Common situations. The rule stated in this Section is commonly applied in two situations, although it is not limited to them. In the first, a party actively hides something from the other, as when the seller of a building paints over a defect. See Illustration 1. In such a case his conduct has the same effect as an assertion that the defect does not exist, and it is therefore a misrepresentation. Similarly, if the offeror reads a written offer to the offeree and omits a portion of it, his conduct has the same effect as an assertion that the omitted portion is not contained in the writing and is therefore a misrepresentation. In the second situation, a party prevents the other from making an investigation that would have disclosed a defect. An analogous situation arises where a party frustrates an investigation made by the other, for example by sending him in search of information where it cannot be found. Even a false denial of knowledge by a party who has possession of the facts may amount to a misrepresentation as to the facts that he knows, just as if he had actually misstated them, if its effect on the other is to lead him to believe that the facts do not exist or cannot be discovered. Action may be considered as likely to prevent another from learning of a fact even though it does not make it impossible to learn of it.

Illustrations:

1. A, seeking to induce B to make a contract to buy his house, paints the basement floor in order to prevent B from discovering that the foundation is cracked. B is prevented from discovering the defect and makes the contract. The concealment is equivalent to an assertion that the foundation is not cracked, and this assertion is a misrepresentation. Whether the contract is voidable by B is determined by the rule stated in § 164.

2. A, seeking to induce B to make a contract to buy his house, convinces C, who, as A knows, is about to tell B that the foundation is cracked, to say nothing to B about the foundation. B is prevented from discovering the defect and makes the contract. A's conduct is equivalent to an assertion

that the foundation is not cracked, and this assertion is a misrepresentation. Whether the contract is voidable by B is determined by the rule stated in § 164.

§ 161. When Non-Disclosure is Equivalent to an Assertion

A person's non-disclosure of a fact known to him is equivalent to an assertion that the fact does not exist in the following cases only:

(a) where he knows that disclosure of the fact is necessary to prevent some previous assertion from being a misrepresentation or from being fraudulent or material.

(b) where he knows that disclosure of the fact would correct a mistake of the other party as to a basic assumption on which that party is making the contract and if non-disclosure of the fact amounts to a failure to act in good faith and in accordance with reasonable standards of fair dealing.

(c) where he knows that disclosure of the fact would correct a mistake of the other party as to the contents or effect of a writing, evidencing or embodying an agreement in whole or in part.

(d) where the other person is entitled to know the fact because of a relation of trust and confidence between them.

Comment:

a. Concealment distinguished. Like concealment, non-disclosure of a fact may be equivalent to a misrepresentation. Concealment necessarily involves an element of non-disclosure, but it is the act of preventing another from learning of a fact that is significant and this act is always equivalent to a misrepresentation (§ 160). Non-disclosure without concealment is equivalent to a misrepresentation only in special situations. A party making a contract is not expected to tell all that he knows to the other party, even if he knows that the other party lacks knowledge on some aspects of the transaction. His nondisclosure, as such, has no legal effect except in the situations enumerated in this Section. He may not, of course, tell half-truths and his assertion of only some of the facts without the inclusion of such additional matters as he knows or believes to be necessary to prevent it from being misleading is itself a misrepresentation. See Comment *a* to § 159. In contrast to the rule applicable to liability in tort for misrepresentation, it is not enough where disclosure is expected, merely to make reasonable efforts to disclose the relevant facts. Actual disclosure is required. . . .

§ 162. When a Misrepresentation is Fraudulent or Material

(1) A misrepresentation is fraudulent if the maker intends his assertion to induce a party to manifest his assent and the maker

(a) knows or believes that the assertion is not in accord with the facts, or

(b) does not have the confidence that he states or implies in the truth of the assertion, or

(c) knows that he does not have the basis that he states or implies for the assertion.

(2) A misrepresentation is material if it would be likely to induce a reasonable person to manifest his assent, or if the maker knows that it would be likely to induce the recipient to do so.

Comment:

a. Meaning of "fraudulent." The word "fraudulent" is used in various senses in the law. In order that a misrepresentation be fraudulent within the meaning of this Section, it must not only be consciously false but must also be intended to mislead another. . . . Consequences are intended if a person either acts with the desire to cause them or acts believing that they are substantially certain to result. . . . Thus one who believes that another is substantially certain to be misled as a result of a misrepresentation intends to mislead even though he may not desire to do so. . . . If the maker knows that his statement is misleading because it is subject to two interpretations, it is fraudulent if he makes it with the intention that it be understood in the false sense. . . . If the recipient continues to rely on a misrepresentation made in an earlier transaction, the misrepresentation is fraudulent if the maker knows that the recipient is still relying. . . . Furthermore, the maker need not have a particular person in mind as the recipient at the time the misrepresentation is made. He may merely have reason to expect that it will reach any of a class of persons, of which the recipient is a member, as in the case of the merchant who furnishes information to a credit agency. See Illustration 1. In order that a fraudulent representation have legal effect within this Chapter, it need not be material. . . . It is, however, essential that it actually induce assent. See §§ 163, 164, 166.

Illustration:

1. A makes to B, a credit rating company, a statement of his financial condition that he knows is untrue, intending that its substance be published to B's subscribers. B summarizes the information and transmits the summary to C, a subscriber. C is thereby induced to make a contract to lend money to A. A's statement is a fraudulent misrepresentation and the contract is voidable by C under the rule stated in § 164.

c. Meaning of "material." Although a fraudulent misrepresentation need not be material in order to entitle the recipient to relief under the rule stated in § 164, a non-fraudulent misrepresentation will not entitle him to relief unless it is material. The materiality of a misrepresentation is determined from the viewpoint of the maker, while the justification of reliance is determined from the viewpoint of the recipient. (Contrast also the concept of a "material" failure to perform. See § 241.) The requirement of materiality may be met in either of two ways. First, a misrepresentation is material if it would be likely to induce a reasonable person to manifest his assent. Second, it is material if the maker knows that for some special reason it is likely to induce the particular recipient to manifest his assent. There may be personal considerations that the recipient regards as important even though they would not be expected to affect others in his situation, and if the maker is aware of this the misrepresentation may be material even though it would not be expected to induce a reasonable person to make the proposed contract. One who preys upon another's known idiosyncrasies cannot complain if the contract is held voidable when he succeeds in what he is endeavoring to accomplish. . . . Although a nonfraudulent misrepresentation that is not material does not make the contract voidable under the rules stated in this Chapter, the recipient may have a claim to relief under other rules, such as those relating to breach of warranty. See Introductory Note to this Topic.

Illustrations:

3. A, while negotiating with B for the sale of A's race horse, tells him that the horse has run a mile in a specified time. A is honestly mistaken, and, unknown to him, the horse has never come close to that time. B is induced by A's assertion to make a contract to buy the horse. A's statement, although not fraudulent, is a material misrepresentation, and the contract is voidable by B under the rule stated in § 164.

4. A, while negotiating with B for the sale of A's race horse, tells him that the horse was bred in a specified stable. A is honestly mistaken, and, unknown to him, it was bred in another stable of better reputation. The specified stable was, unknown to A, founded by B's grandfather, and B is therefore induced by A's assertion to make a contract to buy the horse. A's misrepresentation is neither fraudulent nor material, and the contract is not voidable by B.

5. The facts being otherwise as in Illustration 4, A knows that the named stable was founded by B's grandfather and that B would like to own a horse bred there. A's misrepresentation, although not fraudulent, is material, and the contract is voidable by B under the rule stated in § 164.

§ 163. When a Misrepresentation Prevents Formation of a Contract

If a misrepresentation as to the character or essential terms of a proposed contract induces conduct that appears to be a manifestation of assent by one who neither knows nor has reasonable opportunity to know of the character or essential terms of the proposed contract, his conduct is not effective as a manifestation of assent.

Comment:

a. Rationale. Under the general principle stated in § 19(2), a party's conduct is not effective as a manifestation of his assent unless he knows or has reason to know that the other party may infer from it that he assents. This Section involves an application of that principle where a misrepresentation goes to what is sometimes called the "factum" or the "execution" rather than merely the "inducement." If, because of a misrepresentation as to the character or essential terms of a proposed contract, a party does not know or have reasonable opportunity to know of its character or essential terms, then he neither knows nor has reason to know that the other party may infer from his conduct that he assents to that contract. In such a case there is no effective manifestation of assent and no contract at all. Compare § 174. This result only follows, however, if the misrepresentation relates to the very nature of the proposed contract itself and not merely to one of its nonessential terms. The party may believe that he is not assenting to any contract or that he is assenting to a contract entirely different from the proposed contract. The mere fact that a party is deceived as to the identity of the other party, as when a buyer of goods obtains credit by impersonating a person of means, does not bring the case within the present Section, unless it affects the very nature of the contract. . . . It is immaterial under the rule stated in this Section whether the misrepresentation is made by a party to the transaction or by a third person.

§ 164. When a Misrepresentation Makes a Contract Voidable

(1) If a party's manifestation of assent is induced by either a fraudulent or a material misrepresentation by the other party upon which the recipient is justified in relying, the contract is voidable by the recipient.

(2) If a party's manifestation of assent is induced by either a fraudulent or a material misrepresentation by one who is not a party to the transaction upon which the recipient is justified in relying, the contract is voidable by the recipient, unless the other party to the transaction in good faith and without reason to know of the misrepresentation either gives value or relies materially on the transaction.

Illustrations:

1. A, seeking to induce B to make a contract to buy a tract of land at a price of $1,000 an acre, tells B that the tract contains 100 acres. A knows that it contains only 90 acres. B is induced by the statement to make the contract. Because the statement is a fraudulent misrepresentation (§ 162(1)), the contract is voidable by B, regardless of whether the misrepresentation is material.

2. The facts being otherwise as stated in Illustration 1, A is mistaken and does not know that the tract contains only 90 acres. Because the statement is not a fraudulent misrepresentation, the contract is voidable by B only if the misrepresentation is material (§ 162(2)).

§ 165. Cure by Change of Circumstances

If a contract is voidable because of a misrepresentation and, before notice of an intention to avoid the contract, the facts come into accord with the assertion, the contract is no longer voidable unless the recipient has been harmed by relying on the misrepresentation.

§ 166. When a Misrepresentation as to a Writing Justifies Reformation

If a party's manifestation of assent is induced by the other party's fraudulent misrepresentation as to the contents or effect of a writing evidencing or embodying in whole or in part an agreement, the court at the request of the recipient may reform the writing to express the terms of the agreement as asserted,

(a) if the recipient was justified in relying on the misrepresentation, and

(b) except to the extent that rights of third parties such as good faith purchasers for value will be unfairly affected.

§ 167. When a Misrepresentation is an Inducing Cause

A misrepresentation induces a party's manifestation to assent if it substantially contributes to his decision to manifest his assent.

§ 168. Reliance on Assertions of Opinion

(1) An assertion is one of opinion if it expresses only a belief, without certainty, as to the existence of a fact or expresses only a judgment as to quality, value, authenticity, or similar matters.

(2) If it is reasonable to do so, the recipient of an assertion of a person's opinion as to facts not disclosed and not otherwise known to the recipient may properly interpret it as an assertion

(a) that the facts known to that person are not incompatible with his opinion, or

(b) that he knows facts sufficient to justify him in forming it.

§ 169. When Reliance on an Assertion of Opinion Is Not Justified

To the extent that an assertion is one of opinion only, the recipient is not justified in relying on it unless the recipient

(a) stands in such a relation of trust and confidence to the person whose opinion is asserted that the recipient is reasonable in relying on it, or

(b) reasonably believes that, as compared with himself, the person whose opinion is asserted has special skill, judgment or objectivity with respect to the subject matter, or

(c) is for some other special reason particularly susceptible to a misrepresentation of the type involved.

TOPIC 2. DURESS AND UNDUE INFLUENCE

§ 174. When Duress by Physical Compulsion Prevents Formation of a Contract

If conduct that appears to be a manifestation of assent by a party who does not intend to engage in that conduct is physically compelled by duress, the conduct is not effective as a manifestation of assent.

Comment:

b. "Void" rather than voidable. The distinction between "void contract" and a voidable contract has important consequences. For example, a victim of duress may be held to have ratified the contract if it is voidable, but not if it is "void." Furthermore, a good faith purchaser may acquire good title to property if he takes it from one who obtained voidable title by duress but not if he takes it from one who obtained "void title" by duress. It is immaterial under the rule stated in this Section whether the duress is exercised by a party to the transaction or by a third person. . . .

§ 175. When Duress by Threat Makes a Contract Voidable

(1) If a party's manifestation of assent is induced by an improper threat by the other party that leaves the victim no reasonable alternative, the contract is voidable by the victim.

(2) If a party's manifestation of assent is induced by one who is not a party to the transaction, the contract is voidable by the victim unless the other party to the transaction in good faith and without reason to know of the duress either gives value or relies materially on the transaction.

Comment:

b. No reasonable alternative. A threat, even if improper, does not amount to duress if the victim has a reasonable alternative to succumbing and fails to take advantage of it. It is sometimes said that the threat must arouse such fear as precludes a party from exercising free will and judgment or that it must be such as would induce assent on the part of a brave man or a man of ordinary firmness. The rule stated in this Section omits any such requirement because of its vagueness and impracticability. It is enough if the threat actually induces assent (see Comment *c*) on the part of one who has no reasonable alternative. The alternative may take the form of a legal remedy. For example, the threat of commencing an ordinary civil action to enforce a claim to money may be improper. See § 176(1)(c). However, it does not usually amount to duress because the victim can assert his rights in the threatened action, and this is ordinarily a reasonable alternative to succumbing to the threat, making the proposed contract, and then asserting his rights in a later civil action. See Illustration 1[.] This alternative may not, however, be reasonable if the threat involves, for instance, the seizure of property, the use of oppressive tactics, or the possibility of emotional consequences. See Illustration 2. The standard is a practical one under which account must be taken of the exigencies in which the victim finds himself, and the mere availability of a legal remedy is not controlling if it will not afford effective relief to one in the victim's circumstances. See Illustration[] 4. The alternative to succumbing to the threat need not, however, involve a legal remedy at all. In the case of a threatened denial of needed goods or services, the availability on the market of similar goods or services may afford a reasonable means of avoiding the threat. . . . Since alternative sources of funds are ordinarily available, a refusal to pay money is not duress, absent a showing of peculiar necessity. . . . Where the threat is one of minor vexation only, toleration of the inconvenience involved may be a reasonable alternative. Whether the victim has a reasonable alternative is a mixed question of law and fact, to be answered in clear cases by the court.

Illustrations:

1. A makes an improper threat to commence civil proceedings against B unless B agrees to discharge a claim that B has against A. In order to avoid defending the threatened suit, B is induced to make the contract. Defense of the threatened suit is a reasonable alternative, the threat does not amount to duress, and the contract is not voidable by B.

2. A makes an improper threat to commence a civil action and to file a *lis pendens* against a tract of land owned by B, unless B agrees to discharge a claim that B has against A. Because B is about to make a contract with C for the sale of the land and C refuses to make the contract if the levy is made, B agrees to discharge the claim. B has no reasonable alternative, A's threat is duress, and the contract is voidable by B.

4. A, who has promised B to vacate leased premises in return for $10,000 in order to permit B to demolish the building and construct another, refuses to do so unless B agrees to purchase his worthless furniture for $5,000. B can resort to regular eviction proceedings, but because this will materially delay his construction schedule and cause him heavy financial loss, he is induced by A's threat to make the contract. B has no reasonable alternative, A's threat amounts to duress, and the contract is voidable by B.

§ 176. When a Threat Is Improper

(1) A threat is improper if

(a) what is threatened is a crime or a tort, or the threat itself would be a crime or a tort if it resulted in obtaining property,

(b) what is threatened is a criminal prosecution,

(c) what is threatened is the use of civil process and the threat is made in bad faith, or

(d) the threat is a breach of the duty of good faith and fair dealing under a contract with the recipient.

(2) A threat is improper if the resulting exchange is not on fair terms, and

(a) the threatened act would harm the recipient and would not significantly benefit the party making the threat,

(b) the effectiveness of the threat in inducing the manifestation of assent is significantly increased by prior unfair dealing by the party making the threat, or

(c) what is threatened is otherwise a use of power for illegitimate ends.

Comment:

a. Rationale. An ordinary offer to make a contract commonly involves an implied threat by one party, the offeror, not to make the contract unless his terms are accepted by the other party, the offeree. Such threats are an accepted part of the bargaining process. A threat does not amount to duress unless it is so improper as to amount to an abuse of that process. Courts first recognized as improper threats of physical violence and later included wrongful seizure or detention of goods. Modern decisions have recognized as improper a much broader range of threats, notably those to cause economic harm. The rules stated in this Section recognize as improper both the older categories and their modern extensions under developing notions of "economic duress" or "business compulsion." The fairness of the resulting exchange is often a critical factor in cases involving threats. The categories within Subsection (1) involve threats that are either so shocking that the court will not inquire into the fairness of the resulting exchange (see Clauses (a) and (b)) or that in themselves necessarily involve some element of unfairness (see Clauses (c) and (d)). Those within Subsection (2) involve threats in which the impropriety consists of the threat in combination with resulting unfairness. Such a threat is not improper if it can be shown that the exchange is one on fair terms. Of course a threat may be improper for more than one reason. Any threat that comes within Subsection (1) as well as Subsection (2) is improper without an inquiry, under the rule stated in Subsection (2), into the fairness of the resulting exchange.

e. Breach of contract. A threat by a party to a contract not to perform his contractual duty is not, of itself, improper. Indeed, a modification induced by such a threat may be binding, even in the absence of consideration, if it is fair and equitable in view of unanticipated circumstances. See § 89. The mere fact that the modification induced by the threat fails to meet this test does not mean that the threat is necessarily improper. However, the threat is improper if it amounts to a breach of the duty of good faith and fair dealing imposed by the contract. See § 205. As under the Uniform Commercial Code, the "extortion of a 'modification' without legitimate commercial reason is ineffective as a violation of the duty of good faith. . . . The test of 'good faith' between merchants or as against merchants includes 'observance of reasonable commercial standards of fair dealing in the trade' (Section 2-103), and may in some situations require an objectively demonstrable reason for seeking a modification. But such matters as a market shift which makes performance come to involve a loss may provide such a reason even though there is no such unforeseen difficulty as would make out a legal excuse from performance under Sections 2-615 and 2-616." Comment 2 to Uniform Commercial Code § 2-209. However, a threat of non-performance made for some purpose unrelated to the contract, such as to induce the recipient to make an entirely separate contract, is ordinarily improper. See Illustration 9. Furthermore, a threat may be a breach of the duty of good faith and fair dealing under the contract even though the threatened act is not itself a breach of the contract. See Illustrations 10 and 11. This is particularly likely to be the case if the threat is effective because of power not derived from the contract itself. See Comment *f*.

Illustrations:

8. A contracts to excavate a cellar for B at a stated price. A unexpectedly encounters solid rock and threatens not to finish the excavation unless B modifies the contract to state a new price that is reasonable but is nine times the original price. B, having no reasonable alternative, is induced by A's threat to make the modification by a signed writing that is enforceable by statute without consideration. A's threat is not a breach of his duty of good faith and fair dealing, and the modification is not voidable by B. See Illustration 1 to § 89.

9. A contracts to excavate a cellar for B at a stated price. A begins the excavation and then threatens not to finish it unless B makes a separate contract to excavate the cellar of another building. B, having no reasonable alternative, is induced by A's threat to make the contract. A's threat is a breach of his duty of good faith and fair dealing, and the proposed contract is voidable by B. See Illustration 5 to § 175.

§ 177. When Undue Influence Makes a Contract Voidable

(1) Undue influence is unfair persuasion of a party who is under the domination of the person exercising the persuasion or who by virtue of the relation between them is justified in assuming that that person will not act in a manner inconsistent with his welfare.

(2) If a party's manifestation of assent is induced by undue influence by the other party, the contract is voidable by the victim.

(3) If a party's manifestation of assent is induced by one who is not a party to the transaction, the contract is voidable by the victim unless the other party to the transaction in good faith and without reason to know of the undue influence either gives value or relies materially on the transaction.

CHAPTER 8 UNENFORCEABILITY ON GROUNDS OF PUBLIC POLICY

TOPIC 1. UNENFORCEABILITY IN GENERAL

§ 178. When a Term Is Unenforceable on Grounds of Public Policy

(1) A promise or other term of an agreement is unenforceable on grounds of public policy if legislation provides that it is unenforceable or the interest in

its enforcement is clearly outweighed in the circumstances by a public policy against the enforcement of such terms.

(2) In weighing the interest in the enforcement of a term, account is taken of

(a) the parties' justified expectations,

(b) any forfeiture that would result if enforcement were denied, and

(c) any special public interest in the enforcement of the particular term.

(3) In weighing a public policy against enforcement of a term, account is taken of

(a) the strength of that policy as manifested by legislation or judicial decisions,

(b) the likelihood that a refusal to enforce the term will further that policy,

(c) the seriousness of any misconduct involved and the extent to which it was deliberate, and

(d) the directness of the connection between that misconduct and the term.

Comment:

b. Balancing of interests. Only infrequently does legislation, on grounds of public policy, provide that a term is unenforceable. When a court reaches that conclusion, it usually does so on the basis of a public policy derived either from its own perception of the need to protect some aspect of the public welfare or from legislation that is relevant to that policy although it says nothing explicitly about unenforceability. See § 179. In some cases the contravention of public policy is so grave, as when an agreement involves a serious crime or tort, that unenforceability is plain. In other cases the contravention is so trivial as that it plainly does not preclude enforcement. In doubtful cases, however, a decision as to enforceability is reached only after a careful balancing, in the light of all the circumstances, of the interest in the enforcement of the particular promise against the policy against the enforcement of such terms. The most common factors in the balancing process are set out in Subsections (2) and (3). Enforcement will be denied only if the factors that argue against enforcement clearly outweigh the law's traditional interest in protecting the expectations of the parties, its abhorrence of any unjust enrichment, and any public interest in the enforcement of the particular term.

c. Strength of policy. The strength of the public policy involved is a critical factor in the balancing process. Even when the policy is one manifested by legislation, it may be too insubstantial to outweigh the interest in the enforcement of the term in question. See Illustrations 4 and 5. A court should be particularly alert to this possibility in the case of minor administrative regulations or local ordinances that may not be indicative of the general welfare. A disparity between a relatively modest criminal sanction provided by the legislature and a much larger forfeiture that will result if enforcement of the promise is refused may suggest that the policy is not substantial enough to justify the refusal. See Illustration 4.

Illustrations:

4. A and B make an agreement for the sale of goods for $10,000, in which A promises to deliver the goods in his own truck at a designated time and place. A municipal parking ordinance makes unloading of a truck at that time and place an offense punishable by a fine of up to $50. A delivers the goods to B as provided. Because the public policy manifested by the ordinance is not sufficiently substantial to outweigh the interest in the enforcement of B's promise, enforcement of his promise is not precluded on grounds of public policy.

5. A promises to employ B and B promises to work for A, all work to be done on weekdays. The agreement is made on Sunday in violation of a statute that makes the doing of business on Sunday a misdemeanor. If the court decides that the public policy manifested by the statute is not sufficiently substantial to outweigh the interests in enforcement of A's and B's promises, it will hold that enforcement of their promises is not precluded on grounds of public policy.

§ 179. Bases of Public Policies Against Enforcement

A public policy against the enforcement of promises or other terms may be derived by the court from

(a) legislation relevant to such a policy, or

(b) the need to protect some aspect of the public welfare, as is the case for the judicial policies against, for example,

(i) restraint of trade (§§ 186-188),

(ii) impairment of family relations (§§ 189-191), and

(iii) interference with other protected interests (§§ 192-196, 356).

Comment:

a. Development of the judicial role. Historically, the public policies against enforcement of terms were developed by judges themselves on the basis of their own perception of the need to protect some aspect of the public welfare. Some of these policies are now rooted in precedents accumulated over centuries. Important examples are the policies against restraint of trade, impairment of domestic relations, and interference with duties owed to individuals. These are singled out for mention in Paragraph (b) because they are dealt with in detail in Topics 2-4 of this Chapter. Society has, however, many other interests that are worthy of protection, and as society changes so do these interests. Courts remain alert to other and sometimes novel situations in which enforcement of a term may contravene those interests. At the same time, courts should not implement obsolete policies that have lost their vigor over the course of years. The rule of this Section is therefore an open-ended one that does not purport to exhaust the categories of recognized public policies.

b. Modern role of legislation. The declaration of public policy has now become largely the province of legislators rather than judges. This is in part because legislators are supported by facilities for factual investigations and can be more responsive to the general public. When proscribing conduct, however, legislators seldom address themselves explicitly to the problems of contract law that may arise in connection with such conduct. See § 178(a). Usually they do not even have these problems in mind and say nothing as to the enforceability of terms. In such situations it is pointless to search for the "intention of the legislature," and the court's task is to determine on its own whether it should, by refusing to enforce the promise, add a sanction to those already provided by the legislature. This is a question of "law," in the conventional sense, rather than one of "fact." The legislation is significant, not as controlling the disposition of the case, but as enlightening the court concerning some specific policy to which it is relevant. A court will examine the particular statute in the light of the whole legislative scheme in the jurisdiction to see, for example, if similar statutes in the same area contain explicit provisions making comparable promises unenforceable. It will look to the purpose and history of the statute. The fact that the statute explicitly prohibits the making of a promise or the engaging in the promised conduct may be persuasive in showing a policy against enforcement of a promise but it is not necessarily conclusive. On the other hand, the fact that the statute provides a civil sanction, whether in addition to a criminal penalty or not, may suggest that no other civil sanction such as unenforceability is intended, but this is not necessarily conclusive either. See Illustration 2. Furthermore, even though a field is the subject of legislation, a court may decide that the legislature has not entirely occupied the field and may refuse to enforce a term on grounds of a judicially developed public policy even though there is no contravention of the legislation. The term "legislation" is used here in the same broad sense as in the preceding section. . . . Although no attempt is made in this Restatement to state rules to deal with any of the myriad of specific pieces of legislation that may be involved in such controversies, § 181 deals with the important cases involving licensing requirements.

Illustration:

2. A induces B to make an agreement to buy goods on credit from A by bribing B's purchasing agent. A delivers the goods to B. A state statute makes such bribery a crime and gives B a civil action to recover the amount of the bribe against A. Although the statute already provides for a civil sanction, a court may decide that B's promise to pay the price is unenforceable on grounds of public policy.

CHAPTER 9 THE SCOPE OF CONTRACTUAL OBLIGATIONS

TOPIC 1. THE MEANING OF AGREEMENTS

§ 200. Interpretation of Promise or Agreement

Interpretation of a promise or agreement or a term thereof is the ascertainment of its meaning.

Comment:

a. Formation of contract. Questions of interpretation arise in determining whether there is a contract as well as in determining rights and duties under a contract. Chapter 3 states rules applicable in determining whether the parties have manifested the mutual assent necessary to a contract enforceable as a bargain. The rules stated in the present Topic overlap with those rules, but also apply where the making of a contract is not disputed.

b. Manifestation of intention. As is made clear in Chapter 3, particularly §§ 17-20, the intention of a party that is relevant to formation of a contract is the intention manifested by him rather than any different undisclosed intention. The definitions of "promise," "agreement," and "term" in §§ 2, 3 and 5 also refer to "manifestation of intention." It follows that the meaning of the words or other conduct of a party is not necessarily the meaning he expects or understands. He is not bound by a meaning unless he has reason to know of it, but the expectation and understanding of the other party must also be taken into account. See § 201.

§ 201. Whose Meaning Prevails

(1) Where the parties have attached the same meaning to a promise or agreement or a term thereof, it is interpreted in accordance with that meaning.

(2) Where the parties have attached different meanings to a promise or agreement or a term thereof, it is interpreted in accordance with the meaning attached by one of them if at the time the agreement was made

(a) that party did not know of any different meaning attached by the other, and the other knew the meaning attached by the first party; or

(b) that party had no reason to know of any different meaning attached by the other, and the other had reason to know the meaning attached by the first party.

(3) Except as stated in this Section, neither party is bound by the meaning attached by the other, even though the result may be a failure of mutual assent.

§ 202. Rules in Aid of Interpretation

(1) Words and other conduct are interpreted in the light of all the circumstances, and if the principal purpose of the parties is ascertainable it is given great weight.

(2) A writing is interpreted as a whole, and all writings that are part of the same transaction are interpreted together.

(3) Unless a different intention is manifested,

(a) where language has a generally prevailing meaning, it is interpreted in accordance with that meaning;

(b) technical terms and words of art are given their technical meaning when used in a transaction within their technical field.

(4) Where an agreement involves repeated occasions for performance by either party with knowledge of the nature of the performance and opportunity for objection to it by the other, any course of performance accepted or acquiesced in without objection is given great weight in the interpretation of the agreement.

(5) Wherever reasonable, the manifestations of intention of the parties to a promise or agreement are interpreted as consistent with each other and with any relevant course of performance, course of dealing, or usage of trade.

§ 203. Standards of Preference in Interpretation

In the interpretation of a promise or agreement or a term thereof, the following standards of preference are generally applicable:

(a) an interpretation which gives a reasonable, lawful, and effective meaning to all the terms is preferred to an interpretation which leaves a part unreasonable, unlawful, or of no effect;

(b) express terms are given greater weight than course of performance, course of dealing, and usage of trade, course of performance is given greater weight than course of dealing or usage of trade, and course of dealing is given greater weight than usage of trade;

(c) specific terms and exact terms are given greater weight than general language;

(d) separately negotiated or added terms are given greater weight than standardized terms or other terms not separately negotiated.

§ 204. Supplying an Omitted Essential Term

When the parties to a bargain sufficiently defined to be a contract have not agreed with respect to a term which is essential to a determination of their rights and duties, a term which is reasonable in the circumstances is supplied by the court.

TOPIC 2. CONSIDERATION OF FAIRNESS AND THE PUBLIC INTEREST

§ 205. Duty of Good Faith and Fair Dealing

Every contract imposes upon each party a duty of good faith and fair dealing in its performance and its enforcement.

§206. Interpretation Against the Draftsman

In choosing among the reasonable meanings of a promise or agreement or a term thereof, that meaning is generally preferred which operates against the party who supplies the words or from whom a writing otherwise proceeds.

Comment:

a. Rationale. Where one party chooses the terms of a contract, he is likely to provide more carefully for the protection of his own interests than for those of the other party. He is also more likely than the other party to have reason to know of uncertainties of meaning. Indeed, he may leave meaning deliberately obscure, intending to decide at a later date what meaning to assert. In cases of doubt, therefore, so long as other factors are not decisive, there is substantial reason for preferring the meaning of the other party. The rule is often invoked in cases of standardized contracts and in cases where the drafting party has the stronger bargaining position, but it is not limited to such cases. It is in strictness a rule of legal effect, sometimes called construction, as well as interpretation: its operation depends on the positions of the parties as they appear in litigation, and sometimes the result is hard to distinguish from a denial of effect to an unconscionable clause.

§207. Interpretation Favoring the Public

In choosing among the reasonable meanings of a promise or agreement or a term thereof, a meaning that serves the public interest is generally preferred.

§208. Unconscionable Contract or Term

If a contract or term thereof is unconscionable at the time the contract is made a court may refuse to enforce the contract, or may enforce the remainder of the contract without the unconscionable term, or may so limit the application of any unconscionable term as to avoid any unconscionable result.

Comment:

c. Overall imbalance. Inadequacy of consideration does not of itself invalidate a bargain, but gross disparity in the values exchanged may be an important factor in a determination that a contract is unconscionable and may be sufficient ground, without more, for denying specific performance. See §§ 79, 364. Such a disparity may also corroborate indications of defects in the bargaining process, or may affect the remedy to be granted when there is a violation of a more specific rule. Theoretically it is possible for a contract to be oppressive taken as a whole, even though there is no weakness in the bargaining process and no single term which is in itself unconscionable. Ordinarily, however, an unconscionable contract involves other factors as well as overall imbalance.

d. Weakness in the bargaining process. A bargain is not unconscionable merely because the parties to it are unequal in bargaining position, nor even because the inequality results in an allocation of risks to the weaker party. But gross inequality of bargaining power, together with terms unreasonably favorable to the stronger party, may confirm indications that the transaction involved elements of deception or compulsion, or may show that the weaker party had no meaningful choice, no real alternative, or did not in fact assent or appear to assent to the unfair terms. Factors which may contribute to a finding of unconscionability in the bargaining process include the following: belief by the stronger party that there is no reasonable probability that the weaker party will fully perform the contract; knowledge of the stronger party that the weaker party will be unable to receive substantial benefits from the contract; knowledge of the stronger party that the weaker party is unable reasonably to protect his interests by reason of physical or mental infirmities, ignorance, illiteracy or inability to understand the language of the agreement, or similar factors. . . .

TOPIC 3. EFFECT OF ADOPTION OF A WRITING

§ 209. Integrated Agreements

(1) An integrated agreement is a writing or writings constituting a final expression of one or more terms of an agreement.

(2) Whether there is an integrated agreement is to be determined by the court as a question preliminary to determination of a question of interpretation or to application of the parol evidence rule.

(3) Where the parties reduce an agreement to a writing which in view of its completeness and specificity reasonably appears to be a complete agreement, it is taken to be an integrated agreement unless it is established by other evidence that the writing did not constitute a final expression.

§ 210. Completely and Partially Integrated Agreements

(1) A completely integrated agreement is an integrated agreement adopted by the parties as a complete and exclusive statement of the terms of the agreement.

(2) A partially integrated agreement is an integrated agreement other than a completely integrated agreement.

(3) Whether an agreement is completely or partially integrated is to be determined by the court as a question preliminary to determination of a question of interpretation or to application of the parol evidence rule.

Comment:

a. Complete integration. The definition in Subsection (1) is to be read with the definition of integrated agreement in § 209, to reject the assumption sometimes made that because a writing has been worked out which is final on some matters, it is to be taken as including all the matters agreed upon. Even though there is an integrated agreement, consistent additional terms not reduced to writing may be shown, unless the court finds that the writing was assented to by both parties as a complete and exclusive statement of all the terms. Upon such a finding, however, evidence of the alleged making of consistent additional terms must be kept from the trier of fact. See § 216; Uniform Commercial Code § 2-202 Comment 3.

b. Proof of complete integration. That a writing was or was not adopted as a completely integrated agreement may be proved by any relevant evidence. A document in the form of a written contract, signed by both parties and apparently complete on its face, may be decisive of the issue in the absence of credible contrary evidence. But a writing cannot of itself prove its own completeness, and wide latitude must be allowed for inquiry into circumstances bearing on the intention of the parties.

Illustration:

1. A, a college, owns premises which have no toilet or plumbing facilities or heating equipment. In negotiating a lease to B for use of the premises as a radio station, A orally agrees to permit the use of facilities in an adjacent building and to provide heat. The parties subsequently execute a written lease agreement which makes no mention of facilities or heat. The question whether the written lease was adopted as a completely integrated agreement is to be decided on the basis of all relevant evidence of the prior and contemporaneous conduct and language of the parties.

c. Partial integration. It is often clear from the face of a writing that it is incomplete and cannot be more than a partially integrated agreement. Incompleteness may also be shown by other writings, which may or may not become part of a completely or partially integrated agreement. Or it may be shown by any relevant evidence, oral or written, that an apparently complete writing never became fully effective, or that it was modified after initial adoption.

Illustration:

2. A writes to B a letter offer containing four provisions. B replies by letter that three of the provisions are satisfactory, but makes a counter proposal as to the fourth. After further discussion of the fourth provision, the parties come to oral agreement on a revision of it, but make no further statements as to the other three terms. A's letter is a partially integrated agreement with respect to the first three provisions.

§ 211. Standardized Agreements

(1) Except as stated in Subsection (3), where a party to an agreement signs or otherwise manifests assent to a writing and has reason to believe that like

writings are regularly used to embody terms of agreements of the same type, he adopts the writing as an integrated agreement with respect to the terms included in the writing.

(2) Such a writing is interpreted wherever reasonable as treating alike all those similarly situated, without regard to their knowledge or understanding of the standard terms of the writing.

(3) Where the other party has reason to believe that the party manifesting such assent would not do so if he knew that the writing contained a particular term, the term is not part of the agreement.

§ 212. Interpretation of Integrated Agreement

(1) The interpretation of an integrated agreement is directed to the meaning of the terms of the writing or writings in the light of the circumstances, in accordance with the rules stated in this Chapter.

(2) A question of interpretation of an integrated agreement is to be determined by the trier of fact if it depends on the credibility of extrinsic evidence or on a choice among reasonable inferences to be drawn from extrinsic evidence. Otherwise a question of interpretation of an integrated agreement is to be determined as a question of law.

Comment:

a. "Objective" and "subjective" meaning. Interpretation of contracts deals with the meaning given to language and other conduct by the parties rather than with meanings established by law. But the relevant intention of a party is that manifested by him rather than any different undisclosed intention. In cases of misunderstanding, there may be a contract in accordance with the meaning of one party if the other knows or has reason to know of the misunderstanding and the first party does not. See §§ 200, 201. The meaning of one party may prevail as to one term and the meaning of the other as to another term; thus the contract as a whole may not be entirely in accordance with the understanding of either. When a party is thus held to a meaning of which he had reason to know, it is sometimes said that the "objective" meaning of his language or other conduct prevails over his "subjective" meaning. Even so, the operative meaning is found in the transaction and its context rather than in the law or in the usages of people other than the parties.

b. Plain meaning and extrinsic evidence. It is sometimes said that extrinsic evidence cannot change the plain meaning of a writing, but meaning can almost never be plain except in a context. Accordingly, the rule stated in Subsection (1) is not limited to cases where it is determined that the language used is ambiguous. Any determination of meaning or ambiguity should only be made in the light of the relevant evidence of the situation and relations of the parties, the subject matter of the transaction, preliminary negotiations and statements made therein, usages of trade, and the course of dealing between the parties. See

§§202, 219-23. But after the transaction has been shown in all its length and breadth, the words of an integrated agreement remain the most important evidence of intention. Standards of preference among reasonable meanings are stated in §§203, 206, 207.

Illustrations:

3. A agrees orally with B, a stockbroker, that in transactions between them "abracadabra" shall mean X Company. A sends a signed written order to B to buy 100 shares "abracadabra," and B buys 100 shares of X Company. The parties are bound in accordance with the oral agreement.

4. A and B are engaged in buying and selling shares of stock from each other, and agree orally to conceal the nature of their dealings by using the word "sell" to mean "buy" and using the word "buy" to mean "sell." A sends a written offer to B to "sell" certain shares, and B accepts. The parties are bound in accordance with the oral agreement.

c. Statements of intention. The rule of Subsection (1) permits reference to the negotiations of the parties, including statements of intention and even positive promises, so long as they are used to show the meaning of the writing. A contrary rule in the interpretation of wills is sometimes stated broadly enough to apply to the interpretation of contracts, but that rule is subject to exceptions and rests in part on the more rigorous formal requirements to which wills are subject. Statements of a contracting party subsequent to the adoption of an integration are admissible against him to show his understanding of the meaning asserted by the other party.

d. "Question of law." Analytically, what meaning is attached to a word or other symbol by one or more people is a question of fact. But general usage as to the meaning of words in the English language is commonly a proper subject for judicial notice without the aid of evidence extrinsic to the writing. Historically, moreover, partly perhaps because of the fact that jurors were often illiterate, questions of interpretation of written documents have been treated as questions of law in the sense that they are decided by the trial judge rather than by the jury. Likewise, since an appellate court is commonly in as good a position to decide such questions as the trial judge, they have been treated as questions of law for purposes of appellate review. Such treatment has the effect of limiting the power of the trier of fact to exercise a dispensing power in the guise of a finding of fact, and thus contributes to the stability and predictability of contractual relations. In cases of standardized contracts such as insurance policies, it also provides a method of assuring that like cases will be decided alike.

e. Evaluation of extrinsic evidence. Even though an agreement is not integrated, or even though the meaning of an integrated agreement depends on extrinsic evidence, a question of interpretation is not left to the trier of fact where the evidence is so clear that no reasonable person would determine the issue in any way but one. But if the issue depends on evidence outside the writing, and the possible inferences are conflicting, the choice is for the trier of fact.

§ 213. Effect of Integrated Agreement on Prior Agreements (Parol Evidence Rule)

(1) A binding integrated agreement discharges prior agreements to the extent that it is inconsistent with them.

(2) A binding completely integrated agreement discharges prior agreements to the extent that they are within its scope.

(3) An integrated agreement that is not binding or that is voidable and avoided does not discharge a prior agreement. But an integrated agreement, even though not binding, may be effective to render inoperative a term which would have been part of the agreement if it had not been integrated.

Comment:

a. Parol evidence rule. This Section states what is commonly known as the parol evidence rule. It is not a rule of evidence but a rule of substantive law. Nor is it a rule of interpretation; it defines the subject matter of interpretation. It renders inoperative prior written agreements as well as prior oral agreements. Where writings relating to the same subject matter are assented to as parts of one transaction, both form part of the integrated agreement. Where an agreement is partly oral and partly written, the writing is at most a partially integrated agreement. See § 209.

b. Inconsistent terms. Whether a binding agreement is completely integrated or partially integrated, it supersedes inconsistent terms of prior agreements. To apply this rule, the court must make preliminary determinations that there is an integrated agreement and that it is inconsistent with the term in question. See § 209. Those determinations are made in accordance with all relevant evidence, and require interpretation both of the integrated agreement and of the prior agreement. The existence of the prior agreement may be a circumstance which sheds light on the meaning of the integrated agreement, but the integrated agreement must be given a meaning to which its language is reasonably susceptible when read in the light of all the circumstances. See §§ 212, 214.

c. Scope of a completely integrated agreement. Where the parties have adopted a writing as a complete and exclusive statement of the terms of the agreement, even consistent additional terms are superseded. See § 216. But there may still be a separate agreement between the same parties which is not affected. To apply the rule of Subsection (2) the court in addition to determining that there is an integrated agreement and that it is completely integrated, must determine that the asserted prior agreement is within the scope of the integrated agreement. Those determinations are made in accordance with all relevant evidence, and require interpretation both of the integrated agreement and of the prior agreement.

d. Effect of non-binding integration. An integrated agreement does not supersede prior agreements if it is not binding, for example, by reason of lack of consideration, or if it is voidable and avoided. The circumstances may, however, show an agreement to discharge a prior agreement without regard to whether the integrated agreement is binding, and such an agreement may be effective. Moreover, an integrated agreement may be effective to render inoperative an oral term which would have been part of the agreement if it had not been integrated. The integrated agreement may then be without consideration, even though the inoperative oral term would have furnished consideration.

§214. Evidence of Prior or Contemporaneous Agreements and Negotiations

Agreements and negotiations prior to or contemporaneous with the adoption of a writing are admissible in evidence to establish

(a) that the writing is or is not an integrated agreement;

(b) that the integrated agreement, if any, is completely or partially integrated;

(c) the meaning of the writing, whether or not integrated;

(d) illegality, fraud, duress, mistake, lack of consideration, or other invalidating cause;

(e) ground for granting or denying rescission, reformation, specific performance, or other remedy.

Comment:

a. Integrated agreement and completely integrated agreement. Whether a writing has been adopted as an integrated agreement and, if so, whether the agreement is completely or partially integrated are questions determined by the court preliminary to determination of a question of interpretation or to application of the parol evidence rule. See §§209-13. Writings do not prove themselves; ordinarily, if there is dispute, there must be testimony that there was a signature or other manifestation of assent. The preliminary determination is made in accordance with all relevant evidence, including the circumstances in which the writing was made or adopted. It may require preliminary interpretation of the writing; the court must then consider the evidence which is relevant to the question of interpretation.

b. Interpretation. Words, written or oral, cannot apply themselves to the subject matter. The expressions and general tenor of speech used in negotiations are admissible to show the conditions existing when the writing was made, the application of the words, and the meaning or meanings of the parties. Even though words seem on their face to have only a single possible meaning, other meanings often appear when the circumstances are disclosed. In cases of misunderstanding, there must be inquiry into the meaning attached to the words by each party and into what each knew or had reason to know. See §201.

§215. Contradiction of Integrated Terms

Except as stated in the preceding Section, where there is a binding agreement, either completely or partially integrated, evidence of prior or contemporaneous agreements or negotiations is not admissible in evidence to contradict a term of the writing.

Comment:

a. Relation to other rules. Like § 216, this Section states an evidentiary consequence of § 213. A binding integrated agreement discharges inconsistent prior agreements, and evidence of a prior agreement is therefore irrelevant to the rights of the parties when offered to contradict a term of the writing. The same evidence may be properly considered on the preliminary issues whether there is an integrated agreement and whether it is completely or partially integrated. See §§ 209, 210. If there is a finding that there is an integrated agreement or a completely integrated agreement, the evidence may nevertheless be relevant to a question of interpretation, to a question of invalidating cause, or to a question of remedy. See § 214. But the earlier agreement, no matter how clear, cannot override a later agreement which supersedes or amends it.

b. Interpretation and contradiction. An earlier agreement may help the interpretation of a later one, but it may not contradict a binding later integrated agreement. Whether there is contradiction depends, as is stated in § 213, on whether the two are consistent or inconsistent. This is a question which often cannot be determined from the face of the writing; the writing must first be applied to its subject matter and placed in context. The question is then decided by the court as part of a question of interpretation. Where reasonable people could differ as to the credibility of the evidence offered and the evidence if believed could lead a reasonable person to interpret the writing as claimed by the proponent of the evidence, the question of credibility and the choice among reasonable inferences should be treated as questions of fact. But the asserted meaning must be one to which the language of the writing, read in context, is reasonably susceptible. If no other meaning is reasonable, the court should rule as a matter of law that the meaning is established. See § 212(2).

§ 216. Consistent Additional Terms

(1) Evidence of a consistent additional term is admissible to supplement an integrated agreement unless the court finds that the agreement was completely integrated.

(2) An agreement is not completely integrated if the writing omits a consistent additional agreed term which is

(a) agreed to for separate consideration, or

(b) such a term as in the circumstances might naturally be omitted from the writing.

Comment:

b. Consistency. Terms of prior agreements are superseded to the extent that they are inconsistent with an integrated agreement, and evidence of them is not admissible to contradict a term of the integration. See §§ 213, 215. The determination whether an alleged additional term is consistent or inconsistent with the integrated agreement requires interpretation of the writing in the light of all the circumstances, including the evidence of the additional term. For this purpose, the meaning of the writing includes not only the terms explicitly stated but also those fairly implied as part of the bargain of the parties in fact. It does not include a term supplied by a rule of law designed to fill gaps where the parties have not agreed otherwise, unless it can be inferred that the parties contracted with reference to the rule of law. There is no clear line between implications of fact and rules of law filling gaps; although fairly clear examples of each can be given, other cases will involve almost imperceptible shadings. See § 204.

d. Terms omitted naturally. If it is claimed that a consistent additional term was omitted from an integrated agreement and the omission seems natural in the circumstances, it is not necessary to consider further the questions whether the agreement is completely integrated and whether the omitted term is within its scope, although factual questions may remain. This situation is especially likely to arise when the writing is in a standardized form which does not lend itself to the insertion of additional terms. Thus agreements collateral to a negotiable instrument if written on the instrument might destroy its negotiability or otherwise make it less acceptable to third parties; the instrument may not have space for the additional term. Leases and conveyances are also often in a standard form which leads naturally to the omission of terms which are not standard. These examples are not exclusive. Moreover, there is no rule or policy penalizing a party merely because his mode of agreement does not seem natural to others. Even though the omission does not seem natural, evidence of the consistent additional terms is admissible unless the court finds that the writing was intended as a complete and exclusive statement of the terms of the agreement. See § 210.

e. Written term excluding oral terms ("merger" clause). Written agreements often contain clauses stating that there are no representations, promises or agreements between the parties except those found in the writing. Such a clause may negate the apparent authority of an agent to vary orally the written terms, and if agreed to is likely to conclude the issue whether the agreement is completely integrated. Consistent additional terms may then be excluded even though their omission would have been natural in the absence of such a clause. But such a clause does not control the question whether the writing was assented to as an integrated agreement, the scope of the writing if completely integrated, or the interpretation of the written terms.

§ 217. Integrated Agreement Subject to Oral Requirement of a Condition

Where the parties to a written agreement agree orally that performance of the agreement is subject to the occurrence of a stated condition, the agreement is not integrated with respect to the oral condition.

§ 218. Untrue Recitals; Evidence of Consideration

(1) A recital of a fact in an integrated agreement may be shown to be untrue.
(2) Evidence is admissible to prove whether or not there is consideration for a promise, even though the parties have reduced their agreement to a writing which appears to be a completely integrated agreement.

TOPIC 4. SCOPE AS AFFECTED BY USAGE

§ 219. Usage

Usage is habitual or customary practice.

§ 220. Usage Relevant to Interpretation

(1) An agreement is interpreted in accordance with a relevant usage if each party knew or had reason to know of the usage and neither party knew or had reason to know that the meaning attached by the other was inconsistent with the usage.
(2) When the meaning attached by one party accorded with a relevant usage and the other knew or had reason to know of the usage, the other is treated as having known or had reason to know the meaning attached by the first party.

Illustrations:

4. A and B contract for a year's employment of B by A. As both parties know, there is a usage that such a contract may be terminated by a month's notice. Unless a contrary intention is manifested, the usage is part of the contract.

8. A leases a rabbit warren to B. The written lease contains a covenant that at the end of the term A will buy and B will sell the rabbits at "60£ per thousand." The parties contract with reference to a local usage that 1,000 rabbits means 100 dozen. The usage is part of the contract.

9. In an integrated contract, A promises to sell and B to buy a certain quantity of "white arsenic" for a stated price. The parties contract with reference to a usage of trade that "white arsenic" includes arsenic colored with lamp black. The usage is part of the contract.

§ 221. Usage Supplementing an Agreement

An agreement is supplemented or qualified by a reasonable usage with respect to agreements of the same type if each party knows or has reason to know of the usage and neither party knows or has reason to know that the other party has an intention inconsistent with the usage.

§222. Usage of Trade

(1) A usage of trade is a usage having such regularity of observance in a place, vocation, or trade as to justify an expectation that it will be observed with respect to a particular agreement. It may include a system of rules regularly observed even though particular rules are changed from time to time.

(2) The existence and scope of a usage of trade are to be determined as questions of fact. If a usage is embodied in a written trade code or similar writing the interpretation of the writing is to be determined by the court as a question of law.

(3) Unless otherwise agreed, a usage of trade in the vocation or trade in which the parties are engaged or a usage of trade of which they know or have reason to know gives meaning to or supplements or qualifies their agreement.

§223. Course of Dealing

(1) A course of dealing is a sequence of previous conduct between the parties to an agreement which is fairly to be regarded as establishing a common basis of understanding for interpreting their expressions and other conduct.

(2) Unless otherwise agreed, a course of dealing between the parties gives meaning to or supplements or qualifies their agreement.

TOPIC 5. CONDITIONS AND SIMILAR EVENTS

§224. Condition Defined

A condition is an event, not certain to occur, which must occur, unless its non-occurrence is excused, before performance under a contract becomes due.

Comment:

a. "Condition" limited to event. "Condition" is used in this Restatement to denote an event which qualifies a duty under a contract. It is recognized that "condition" is used with a wide variety of other meanings in legal discourse. . . . For the sake of precision, "condition" is not used here in these other senses.

Illustration:

1. A contracts to sell and B to buy goods pursuant to a writing which provides, under the heading "Conditions of Sale," that "the obligations of the parties are conditional on B obtaining from X Bank by June 30 a letter of credit" on stated terms. The quoted language is a term of the agreement (§ 5), not a condition. The event referred to by the term, obtaining the letter of credit by June 30, is a condition.

b. Uncertainty of event. Whether the reason for making an event a condition is to shift to the obligee the risk of its non-occurrence, or whether it is to induce the obligee to cause the event to occur (see Introductory Note to this Topic), there is inherent in the concept of condition some degree of uncertainty as to the occurrence of the event. Therefore, the mere passage of time, as to which there is no uncertainty, is not a condition and a duty is unconditional if nothing but the passage of time is necessary to give rise to a duty of performance. Moreover, an event is not a condition, even though its occurrence is uncertain, if it is referred to merely to measure the passage of time after which an obligor is to perform. . . . Performance under a contract becomes due when all necessary events, including any conditions and the passage of any required time, have occurred so that a failure of performance will be a breach. See §§ 231-43.

The event need not, in order to be a condition, be one that is to occur after the making of the contract, although that is commonly the case. It may relate to the present or even to the past, as is the case where a marine policy insures against a loss that may already have occurred. Furthermore, a duty may be conditioned upon the failure of something to happen rather than upon its happening, and in that case its failure to happen is the event that is the condition.

Illustration:

2. A tells B, "If you will paint my house, I will pay you $1,000 on condition that 30 days have passed after you have finished." B paints A's house. Although A is not under a duty to pay B $1,000 until 30 days have passed, the passage of that time is not a condition of A's duty to pay B $1,000.

§ 225. Effects of the Non-Occurrence of a Condition

(1) Performance of a duty subject to a condition cannot become due unless the condition occurs or its non-occurrence is excused.

(2) Unless it has been excused, the non-occurrence of a condition discharges the duty when the condition can no longer occur.

(3) Non-occurrence of a condition is not a breach by a party unless he is under a duty that the condition occur.

Comment:

a. Two effects. The unexcused non-occurrence of a condition has two possible effects on the duty subject to that condition. The first effect always follows and the second often does. The first, stated in Subsection (1), is that of preventing performance of the duty from becoming due. This follows from the definition of "condition" in § 224. Performance of the duty may still become due, however, if the condition occurs later within the time for its occurrence. The non-occurrence of the condition within that time has the additional effect, stated in Subsection (2), of discharging the duty. The time within which the condition can occur in order for the performance of the duty to become due may be fixed by a term of the agreement or, in the absence of such a term, by one supplied by the court (§ 204). Where discharge would produce harsh results, this second effect may be avoided by rules of interpretation (§§ 226, 228) or of excuse of conditions (Comment *b* and § 229).

Illustration:

2. B gives A $10,000 to use in perfecting an invention, and A promises to repay it only out of royalties received during his lifetime from the sale of the patent rights. In spite of diligent efforts, A is unable to perfect his invention and obtain a patent, and no royalties are received. A dies after six years. B has no claim against A's estate. Receipt of royalties is a condition of A's duty to repay the money and A's duty is discharged by the non-occurrence of that condition during his lifetime.

b. Excuse. The non-occurrence of a condition of a duty is said to be "excused" when the condition need no longer occur in order for performance of the duty to become due. The non-occurrence of a condition may be excused on a variety of grounds. It may be excused by a subsequent promise, even without consideration, to perform the duty in spite of the non-occurrence of the condition. See the treatment of "waiver" in § 84, and the treatment of discharge in §§ 273-[281, and 283]. It may be excused by acceptance of performance in spite of the non-occurrence of the condition, or by rejection following its non-occurrence accompanied by an inadequate statement of reasons. See §§ 246-48. It may be excused by a repudiation of the conditional duty or by a manifestation of an inability to perform it. See § 255; §§ 250-51. It may be excused by prevention or hindrance of its occurrence through a breach of the duty of good faith and fair dealing (§ 205). See § 239. And it may be excused by impracticability. See § 271. These and other grounds for excuse are dealt with in other chapters of this Restatement. This Chapter deals only with one general ground, excuse to avoid forfeiture. See § 229.

c. Effect of excuse. When the non-occurrence of a condition of a duty is excused, the damages for breach of the duty will depend on whether or not the occurrence of the condition was also part of the performances to be exchanged under the exchange of promises. If it was not part of the agreed exchange, the obligor is liable for the same damages for which he would have been liable had the duty originally been unconditional. If it was part of the agreed exchange, however, the saving to the obligee resulting from the non-occurrence of the condition must be subtracted in determining the obligor's liability for damages. Rules for determining damages are set out in § 347; see generally §§ 346-56. If the obligee is under a duty that the condition occur, the ground for the excuse of the non-occurrence of the condition may not be a ground for discharge of that duty. He may therefore be liable for breach of the duty in spite of the excuse of the non-occurrence of the condition. Not only may a party excuse entirely the non-occurrence of a condition of his duty, but he may merely excuse its non-occurrence during the period of time in which it would otherwise have to occur. If he does this, the non-occurrence of the condition during that period will not discharge the duty under Subsection (2), although its non-occurrence will ultimately have that effect. . . .

Illustration:

3. A contracts with B to build a house for $50,000, payable on condition that A present a certificate from C, B's architect, showing that the work has been properly completed. A properly completes the work, but C refuses to give the certificate because of collusion with B, and the non-occurrence of the condition is therefore excused. See § 239. Since the presentation of the architect's certificate is not part of the performances to be exchanged under the exchange of promises, A has a claim against B for $50,000.

d. Imposition of duty distinguished. When one party chooses to use the institution of contract to induce the other party to cause an event to occur, he may do so by making the event a condition of his own duty (Introductory Note to this Topic). Or he may do so by having the other party undertake a duty that the event occur. Or he may do both. But, as Subsection (3) makes clear, a term making an event a condition of an obligor's duty does not of itself impose a duty on the obligee and the non-occurrence of the event is not of itself a breach by the obligee. Unless the obligee is under such a duty, the non-occurrence of the event gives rise to no claim against him. The same term may, however, be interpreted not only to make an event a condition of the obligor's duty, but also to impose a duty on the obligee that it occur. And even where no term of the agreement imposes a duty that a condition occur, the court may supply such a term. See § 204.

Illustrations:

6. A, a shipowner, promises to carry B's cargo on his ship to Portsmouth. B promises to pay A the stipulated freight on condition that A's ship sail directly there on its next sailing. A's ship carries B's cargo to Portsmouth, but puts into port on the way. Since carrying B's cargo directly to Portsmouth is a condition of B's duty, no duty to pay arises, and, since the condition can no longer occur, B's duty is discharged. Since A is under no duty to carry B's cargo directly to Portsmouth, however, his failure to do so is not a breach.

7. The facts being otherwise as stated in Illustration 6, A promises to carry B's cargo on his ship directly to Portsmouth on its next sailing. Since carrying B's cargo directly to Portsmouth is a condition of B's duty, no duty to pay arises and, since the condition can no longer occur, B's duty is discharged. Since A is under a duty to carry B's cargo directly to Portsmouth, his failure to do so is also a breach.

e. Ignorance immaterial. The rules stated in this Section apply without regard to whether a party knows or does not know of the non-occurrence of a condition of his duty.

§226. How an Event May Be Made a Condition

An event may be made a condition either by the agreement of the parties or by a term supplied by the court.

Comment:

c. By a term supplied by court. When the parties have omitted a term that is essential to a determination of their rights and duties, the court may supply a term which is reasonable in the circumstances (§ 204). Where that term makes an event a condition, it is often described as a "constructive" (or "implied in law") condition. This serves to distinguish it from events which are made conditions by the agreement of the parties, either by their words or by other conduct, and which are described as "express" and as "implied in fact" (inferred from fact) conditions. See Comments *a* and *b* to § 4. It is useful to distinguish "constructive" conditions, even though the distinction is necessarily somewhat arbitrary. For one thing, it is helpful in analysis and description to have terminology that reflects the two distinctive processes, sometimes called "interpretation" and "construction," that give rise to conditions. See Uniform Commercial Code §§ 2-313 to 2-315, in which an analogous distinction is made between express and implied warranties. For another, to the extent that the parties have, by a term of their agreement, clearly made an event a condition, they can be confident that a court will ordinarily feel constrained strictly to apply that term, while the same court may regard itself as having considerable latitude in tailoring a similar term that it has itself supplied.

One example of such a term supplied by the court is the requirement of § 45(2) that the offeree, under an option contract, complete or tender the invited performance as a condition of the offeror's duty. A more common example occurs where an obligor's duty cannot be performed without some act by the obligee, and the court supplies a term making that act a condition of the obligor's duty. In most such situations, the obligee's own obligation of good faith and fair dealing (§ 205) imposes on him a duty to do the act, so that a material failure to perform that duty would, in any case, have the same effect as the non-occurrence of a condition under the rules relating to performances to be exchanged under an exchange of promises (§ 239). The examples given in the following illustrations involve situations where no duty to do the act is imposed.

Illustration:

7. A promises to make necessary interior repairs on a building that he has leased to B, but reserves no privilege of entering the building. B's giving reasonable notice to A of any necessary interior repairs of which A would otherwise be unaware is a condition of A's duty to make those repairs, although B is under no duty to give notice.

§227. Standards of Preference with Regard to Conditions

(1) In resolving doubts as to whether an event is made a condition of an obligor's duty, and as to the nature of such an event, an interpretation is

preferred that will reduce the obligee's risk of forfeiture, unless the event is within the obligee's control or the circumstances indicate that he has assumed the risk.

(2) Unless the contract is a type under which only one party generally undertakes duties, when it is doubtful whether

(a) a duty is imposed on an obligee that an event occur, or

(b) the event is made a condition of the obligor's duty, or

(c) the event is made a condition of the obligor's duty and a duty is imposed on the obligee that the event occur,

The first interpretation is preferred if the event is within the obligee's control.

(3) In case of doubt, an interpretation under which an event is a condition of an obligor's duty is preferred over an interpretation under which the non-occurrence of the event is a ground for discharge of that duty after it has become a duty to perform.

§ 228. Satisfaction of the Obligor as a Condition

When it is a condition of an obligor's duty that he be satisfied with respect to the obligee's performance or with respect to something else, and it is practicable to determine whether a reasonable person in the position of the obligor would be satisfied, an interpretation is preferred under which the condition occurs if such a reasonable person in the position of the obligor would be satisfied.

Comment:

a. Conditions of satisfaction. This Section sets out a special standard of preference for a type of condition that has long been of particular interest and importance—the satisfaction of the obligor himself, rather than a third party. Usually it is the obligee's performance as to which the obligor is to be satisfied, but it may also be something else, such as the propitiousness of circumstances for his enterprise. The agreement will often use language such as "satisfaction" or "complete satisfaction," without making it clear that the test is merely one of honest satisfaction rather than of reasonable satisfaction. Under any interpretation, the exercise of judgment must be in accordance with the duty of good faith and fair dealing (§ 205), and for this reason, the agreement is not illusory (§ 77). If the agreement leaves no doubt that it is only honest satisfaction that is meant and no more, it will be so interpreted, and the condition does not occur if the obligor is honestly, even though unreasonably, dissatisfied. Even so, the dissatisfaction must be with the circumstance and not with the bargain and the mere statement of the obligor that he is not satisfied is not conclusive on the question of his honest satisfaction.

Illustration:

2. A contracts to sell and B to buy 500 barrels of cherries in syrup "quality to be satisfactory in buyer's honest judgment," delivery to be in

installments. After deliveries of and payments for a total of 100 barrels, B states that he is not satisfied and refuses to take more. Since the agreement clearly provides a test of honest satisfaction, B's termination is effective if his judgment is in fact made honestly in accordance with his duty of good faith and fair dealing (§ 205). However, A may show that B's rejection was for other reasons by proving, for example, that B expressed satisfaction at the time of the first deliveries, that B's demand had dropped sharply, and that A's cherries are selected and put up with great care and are of the highest quality.

b. Preference for objective standard. When, however, the agreement does not make it clear that it requires merely honest satisfaction, it will not usually be supposed that the obligee has assumed the risk of the obligor's unreasonable, even if honest, dissatisfaction. In such a case, to the extent that it is practicable to apply an objective test of reasonable satisfaction, such a test will be applied. The situation differs from that where the satisfaction of a third party such as an architect, surveyor or engineer is concerned. . . . These professionals, even though employed by the obligor, are assumed to be capable of independent judgment, free from the selfish interests of the obligor. But if the obligor would subject the obligee's right to compensation to his own idiosyncrasies, he must use clear language. When, as is often the case, the preferred interpretation will reduce the obligee's risk of forfeiture, so that § 227(1) also applies, there is an additional argument in its favor. This argument is particularly strong where the obligor will be left with a benefit which he cannot return. If, however, the circumstance with respect to which a party is to be satisfied is such that the application of an objective test is impracticable, the rule of this Section is not applicable. A court will then, for practical reasons, apply a subjective test of honest satisfaction, even if the agreement admits of doubt on the point and even if the result will be to increase the obligee's risk of forfeiture.

Illustrations:

3. A contracts with B to install a heating system in B's factory, for a price of $20,000 to be paid "on condition of satisfactory completion." A installs the heating system, but B states that he is not satisfied with it and refuses to pay the $20,000. B gives no reason except that he does not approve of the heating system, and according to experts in the field the system as installed is entirely satisfactory. A has a claim against B for $20,000 since it is practicable to apply an objective test to the installation of the heating system. This interpretation is also preferred because it reduces A's risk of forfeiture.

4. A contracts with B to paint a portrait of B's daughter, for which B promises to pay $5,000 "if entirely satisfied." A paints the portrait, but B honestly states that he is not satisfied with it and refuses to pay the $5,000. B gives no reason except that the portrait does not please him, and according to experts in the field the portrait is an admirable work of art. A has no claim against B since it is not practicable to apply an objective test to the painting.

§ 229. Excuse of a Condition to Avoid Forfeiture

To the extent that the non-occurrence of a condition would cause disproportionate forfeiture, a court may excuse the non-occurrence of that condition unless its occurrence was a material part of the agreed exchange.

§ 230. Event That Terminates a Duty

(1) Except as stated in Subsection (2), if under the terms of the contract the occurrence of an event is to terminate an obligor's duty of immediate performance or one to pay damages for breach, that duty is discharged if the event occurs.

(2) The obligor's duty is not discharged if occurrence of the event

(a) is the result of a breach by the obligor of his duty of good faith and fair dealing, or

(b) could not have been prevented because of impracticability and continuance of the duty does not subject the obligor to a materially increased burden.

(3) The obligor's duty is not discharged if, before the event occurs, the obligor promises to perform the duty even if the event occurs and does not revoke his promise before the obligee materially changes his position in reliance on it.

CHAPTER 10 PERFORMANCE AND NON-PERFORMANCE

TOPIC 1. PERFORMANCES TO BE EXCHANGED UNDER AN EXCHANGE OF PROMISES

§ 234. Order of Performances

(1) Where all or part of the performances to be exchanged under an exchange of promises can be rendered simultaneously, they are to that extent due simultaneously, unless the language or the circumstances indicate the contrary.

(2) Except to the extent stated in Subsection (1), where the performance of only one party under such an exchange requires a period of time, his performance is due at an earlier time than that of the other party, unless the language or the circumstances indicate the contrary.

Comment:

a. Advantages of simultaneous performance. A requirement that the parties perform simultaneously where their performances are to be exchanged under an exchange of promises is fair for two reasons. First, it offers both parties maximum security against disappointment of their expectations of a subsequent exchange of performances by allowing each party to defer his own performance until he has been assured that the other will perform. This advantage is implemented by the rule stated in § 238, which deals with offers to perform. Second, it avoids placing on either party the burden of financing the other before the latter has performed. Subsection (1) therefore imposes a requirement of simultaneous performance whenever this is feasible under the contract, in the absence of language or circumstances indicating a contrary intention. . . . Even absent an express provision, a contrary intention may be shown by circumstances including usage of trade and course of dealing (§§ 221, 223; Uniform Commercial Code § 1-205).

b. When simultaneous performance possible under agreement. In the absence of language or circumstances showing a contrary intention, the requirement of simultaneous performance stated in Subsection (1) applies whenever such performance is possible, consistent with the terms of the contract. . . . Cases in which simultaneous performance is possible under the terms of the contract can be grouped into five categories: (1) where the same time is fixed for the performance of each party; (2) where a time is fixed for the performance of one of the parties and no time is fixed for the other; (3) where no time is fixed for the performance of either party; (4) where the same period is fixed within which each party is to perform; (5) where different periods are fixed within which each party is to perform. The requirement of simultaneous performance applies to the first four categories. The requirement does not apply to the fifth category, even if simultaneous performance is possible, because in fixing different periods for performance the parties must have contemplated the possibility of performance at different times under their agreement. Therefore in cases in the fifth category the circumstances show an intention contrary to the rule stated in Subsection (1).

Illustrations:

1. A promises to sell land to B, delivery of the deed to be on July 1. B promises to pay A $50,000, payment to be made on July 1. Delivery of the deed and payment of the price are due simultaneously.

2. A promises to sell land to B, the deed to be delivered on July 1. B promises to pay A $50,000, no provision being made for the time of payment. Delivery of the deed and payment of the price are due simultaneously.

3. A promises to sell land to B and B promises to pay A $50,000, no provision being made for the time either of delivery of the deed or of payment. Delivery of the deed and payment of the price are due simultaneously.

4. A promises to sell land to B, delivery of the deed to be on or before July 1. B promises to pay A $50,000, payment to be on or before July 1. Delivery of the deed and payment of the price are due simultaneously.

5. A promises to sell land to B, delivery of the deed to be on or before July 1. B promises to pay A $50,000, payment to be on or before August 1. Delivery of the deed and payment of the prices are not due simultaneously.

c. When simultaneous performance possible in part. The requirement of simultaneous performance stated in Subsection (1) also applies where only part rather than all of the performance of one party can be performed simultaneously with either part or all of the performance of the other party. . . .

Illustration:

7. A promises to sell land to B, delivery of the deed to be one year from July 1. B promises to pay A $50,000 in installments of $10,000 on each July 1 for five years. Delivery of the deed and payment of the second installment are due simultaneously.

e. Where performance requires a period of time. Where the performance of one party requires a period of time and the performance of the other party does not, their performance cannot be simultaneous. Since one of the parties must perform first, he must forego the security that a requirement of simultaneous performance affords against disappointment of his expectation of an exchange of performances, and he must bear the burden of financing the other party before the latter has performed. See Comment *a.* Of course the parties can by express provision mitigate the harshness of a rule that requires that one completely perform before the other performs at all. They often do this, for example, in construction contracts by stating a formula under which payment is to be made at stated intervals as work progresses. But it is not feasible for courts to devise such formulas for the wide variety of such cases that come before them in which the parties have made no provision. Centuries ago, the principle became settled that where work is to be done by one party and payment is to be made by the other, the performance of the work must precede payment, in the absence of a showing of a contrary intention. It is sometimes supposed, that this principle grew out of employment contracts, and reflects a conviction that employers as a class are more likely to be responsible than are workmen paid in advance. Whether or not the explanation is correct, most parties today contract with reference to the principle, and unless they have evidenced a contrary intention it is at least as fair as the opposite rule would be.

f. Applicability of rule. The rule stated in Subsection (2) usually finds its application to contracts involving services, such as construction and employment contracts. The common practice of making express provision for progress payments has diminished its importance with regard to the former, and the widespread enactment of state wage statutes giving the employee a right to the frequent periodic payment of wages has lessened its significance with regard to the latter. Nevertheless, it is a helpful rule for residual cases not otherwise provided for. It applies not only to contracts under which the performance of one party is more or less continuous, but also to contracts where performance consists of a series of acts with an interval of time between them. See Comment *c*. Under a contract of the latter type, simultaneity may be possible in part and, to the extent that it is possible, the rule stated in Subsection (2) is subject to that stated in Subsection (1). See Illustrations 6 and 12.

TOPIC 2. EFFECT OF PERFORMANCE AND NON-PERFORMANCE

§235. Effect of Performance as Discharge and of Non-Performance as Breach

(1) Full performance of a duty under a contract discharges the duty.

(2) When performance of a duty under a contract is due any non-performance is a breach.

§237. Effect on Other Party's Duties of a Failure to Render Performance

Except as stated in §240, it is a condition of each party's remaining duties to render performances to be exchanged under an exchange of promises that there be no uncured material failure by the other party to render any such performance due at an earlier time.

Comment:

a. Effect of non-occurrence of condition. Under the rule stated in this Section, a material failure of performance, including defective performance as well as an absence of performance, operates as the non-occurrence of a condition. Under §225, the non-occurrence of a condition has two possible effects on the duty subject to that condition. See Comment *a* to §225. The first is that of preventing performance of the duty from becoming due, at least temporarily (§225(1)). The second is that of discharging the duty when the condition can no longer occur (§225(2)). A material failure of performance has, under this Section, these effects on the other party's remaining duties of performance with respect to the exchange. It prevents performance of those duties from becoming due, at least temporarily, and it discharges those duties if it has not been cured during the time in which performance can occur. The occurrence of conditions of the type dealt with in this Section is required out of a sense of fairness rather than as a result of the agreement of the parties. Such conditions are therefore sometimes referred to as "constructive conditions of exchange." Cf. §204. What is sometimes referred to as a "failure of consideration" by courts and statutes . . . is referred to in this Restatement as "failure of performance" to avoid confusion with the absence of consideration. Circumstances significant in determining whether a failure is material are set out in §241. Circumstances significant in determining the period of time after which remaining duties are discharged, if a material failure has not been cured, are set out in §242. The rules stated in this Section and the one following apply without regard to whether or not the failure of performance is a breach. They apply, for example, even though the failure is justified on the ground of impracticability of performance (Chapter 11). Illustrations of the operation of these rules in situations in which the failure is justified are given in other chapters under the sections that deal with the particular justification, such as impracticability. See, e.g., §§ 267, 268. The illustrations in this Chapter concern, for the most part, their operation in situations where the failure is a breach. . . . The rules of this Section and the one following apply even when the promise of the party in default is unenforceable under the Statute of Frauds, while the promise of the other party is enforceable. See § 140. They are, of course, subject to variation by agreement of the parties.

Illustration:

1. A contracts to build a house for B for $50,000, progress payments to be made monthly in an amount equal to 85% of the price of the work performed during the preceding month, the balance to be paid on the architect's certificate of satisfactory completion of the house. Without justification B fails to make a $5,000 progress payment. A thereupon stops work on the house and a week goes by. A's failure to continue the work is not a breach and B has no claim against A. B's failure to make the progress payment is an uncured material failure of performance which operates as the non-occurrence of a condition of A's remaining duties of performance under the exchange. If B offers to make the delayed payment and in all the circumstances it is not too late to cure the material breach, A's duties to continue the work are not discharged. A has a claim against B for damages for partial breach because of the delay.

b. First material failure of performance. In many disputes over failure of performance, both parties fail to finish performance, and the question is whether one of them is justified in so doing by the other party's failure. (Compare Comment *d.*) This Section states the fundamental rule under which that question is to be answered. (The liability of the other party for damages for total breach is governed by the rule stated in § 243.) The rule is based on the principle that where performances are to be exchanged under an exchange of promises, each party is entitled to the assurance that he will not be called upon to perform his remaining duties of performance with respect to the expected exchange if there has already been an uncured material failure of performance by the other party. The central problem is in determining which party is chargeable with the first uncured material failure of performance. In determining the relative times when performance is due, the terms of the agreement and the supplementary rules on time for performance should be considered (§§ 233, 234). In determining whether there has been a failure of performance, the terms of the agreement and the supplementary rules such as those on omitted essential terms (§ 204) and the duty of good faith and fair dealing (§ 205) should be considered. In determining whether a failure of performance is material, the circumstances listed in § 241 should be considered. Even if the failure is material, it may still be possible to cure it by subsequent performance without a material failure. In the event of cure the injured party may still have a claim for any remaining non-performance as well as for any delay. In determining when it is too late to cure a failure of performance, the circumstances listed in § 242 should be considered. In making all of these determinations the situation of the parties is to be viewed as of the time for performance and in terms of the actual failure. If, for example, under the terms of the agreement the order of performance depends on an event subsequent to the time of the making of the contract, that event is to be taken into account.

d. Substantial performance. In an important category of disputes over failure of performance, one party asserts the right to payment on the ground that he has completed his performance, while the other party refuses to pay on the ground that there is an uncured material failure of performance. (Compare Comment *b.*) A typical example is that of the building contractor who claims from the owner payment of the unpaid balance under a construction contract. In such cases it is common to state the issue, not in terms of whether there has been an uncured material failure by the contractor, but in terms of whether there has been substantial performance by him. This manner of stating the issue does not change its substance, however, and the rule stated in this Section also applies to such cases. If there has been substantial although not full performance, the building contractor has a claim for the unpaid balance and the owner has a claim only for damages. If there has not been substantial performance, the building contractor has no claim for the unpaid balance, although he may have a claim in restitution (§ 374). The considerations in determining whether performance is substantial are those listed in § 241 for determining whether a failure is material. . . . If, however, the parties have made an event a condition of their agreement, there is no mitigating standard of materiality or substantiality applicable to the non-occurrence of that event. If, therefore, the agreement makes full performance a condition, substantial performance is not sufficient and if relief is to be had under the contract, it must be through excuse of the non-occurrence of the condition to avoid forfeiture. See § 229[.]

Illustration:

11. A contracts to build a house for B, for which B promises to pay $50,000 in monthly progress payments equal to 85% of the value of the work with the balance to be paid on completion. When A completes construction, B refuses to pay the $7,500 balance claiming that there are defects that amount to an uncured material breach. If the breach is material, A's performance is not substantial and he has no claim under the contract against B, although he may have a claim in restitution (§ 374). If the breach is not material, A's performance is said to be substantial, he has a claim under the contract against B for $7,500, and B has a claim against A for damages because of the defects.

§ 238. Effect on Other Party's Duties of a Failure to Offer Performance

Where all or part of the performances to be exchanged under an exchange of promises are due simultaneously, it is a condition of each party's duties to render such performance that the other party either render or, with manifested present ability to do so, offer performance of his part of the simultaneous exchange.

§ 239. Effect on Other Party's Duties of a Failure Justified by Non-Occurrence of a Condition

(1) A party's failure to render or to offer performance may, except as stated in Subsection (2), affect the other party's duties under the rules stated in §§ 237 and 238 even though failure is justified by the non-occurrence of a condition.

(2) The rule stated in Subsection (1) does not apply if the other party assumed the risk that he would have to perform in spite of such a failure.

§ 240. Part Performances as Agreed Equivalents

If the performances to be exchanged under an exchange of promises can be apportioned into corresponding pairs of part performances so that the parts of each pair are properly regarded as agreed equivalents, a party's performance of his part of such a pair has the same effect on the other's duties to render performance of the agreed equivalent as it would have if only that pair of performances had been promised.

Comment:

d. Apportionment. The rule stated in this Section cannot be applied unless the parties' performances can be apportioned into corresponding pairs of part performances. The process of apportionment is essentially one of calculation and the rule can only be applied where calculation is feasible. It is enough, however, if the price of separate items is separately stated in the agreement itself or in a price list on which the agreement was based, or can be reliably ascertained from stated prices for components or from a total price for similar items.

Illustration:

4. A contracts with B to work for one year as a real estate salesman and to devote his full time to this work. A is to receive half of the real estate commission on all sales that he effects. A devotes full time to this work for ten months, but unjustifiably devotes only part time for the last two months. A court may apportion the unpaid commissions earned by A into those earned during the first ten months and those earned under the last two months according to the formula stated in the contract and, if it finds that working full time for ten months and the commissions on the sales over those months are agreed equivalents, A can recover the unpaid commissions for those months under the contract. B then has a claim against A for damages for his failure to devote full time during the last two months.

e. Agreed equivalents. The corresponding pairs of performances so apportioned only come within the rule stated in this Section if it is proper to regard the parts of each pair as agreed equivalents. . . . The standard under this Section, like that of materiality under § 237, is necessarily a somewhat imprecise and flexible one. It requires that the parts of a pair be of roughly equivalent value to the injured party in terms of his expectation with respect to the total agreed exchange. This is because fairness requires that a party, having received only a fraction of the performance that he expected under a contract, not be asked to pay an identical fraction of the price that he originally promised on the expectation of full performance, unless it appears that the performance that he actually received is worth to him roughly that same fraction of what full performance would have been worth to him. Therefore the mere fact that the subject of the contract is sold by weight or measure and the total price determined by a unit price (e.g., per pound or cubic yard or acre) does not result in agreed equivalents. The injured party will not be required to pay for a part of the performance that he has received if he cannot make full use of that part without the remainder of the performance, as, for example, where a buyer has received a machine but not an attachment necessary for its operation. In deciding whether the injured party can make full use of only part, a court must, of course, take account of the possibility that the remainder of the performance can be easily obtained from some other source, as, for example, where the attachment is available on the market.

Illustration:

8. A contracts with B to drive 10,000 logs from various points down a river to B's boom at one cent per log mile. Because of a flood, A drives only 5,763 logs an average distance of 100 miles each to B's boom, and leaves the other 4,237 logs on the banks part of the way to B's boom. B expects to resell the logs and can resell the 5,763 at the same unit price as the entire 10,000. The driving of the logs to B's boom and the corresponding price at the contract rate are agreed equivalents, but the driving of logs part way and the corresponding price at the contract rate are not. A can recover $5,763 under the contract for the 5,763 logs that he has driven to B's boom, but can recover nothing for the remaining 4,237 logs that he has driven only part of the way. If A's failure to drive the remaining logs to B's boom is unjustified, it is a breach, and B has a claim against A for damages. Whether A's failure is justified on the ground of impracticability of performance is determined under the rules stated in §§ 261 and 263.

§ 241. Circumstances Significant in Determining Whether a Failure Is Material

In determining whether a failure to render or to offer performance is material, the following circumstances are significant:

(a) the extent to which the injured party will be deprived of the benefit which he reasonably expected;

(b) the extent to which the injured party can be adequately compensated for the part of that benefit of which he will be deprived;

(c) the extent to which the party failing to perform or to offer to perform will suffer forfeiture;

(d) the likelihood that the party failing to perform or to offer to perform will cure his failure, taking account of all the circumstances including any reasonable assurances;

(e) the extent to which the behavior of the party failing to perform or to offer to perform comports with standards of good faith and fair dealing.

§ 243. Effect of a Breach by Non-Performance as Giving Rise to a Claim for Damages for Total Breach

(1) With respect to performances to be exchanged under an exchange of promises, a breach by non-performance gives rise to a claim for damages for total breach only if it discharges the injured party's remaining duties to render such performance, other than a duty to render an agreed equivalent under § 240.

(2) Except as stated in Subsection (3), a breach by non-performance accompanied or followed by a repudiation gives rise to a claim for damages for total breach.

(3) Where at the time of the breach the only remaining duties of performance are those of the party in breach and are for the payment of money in installments not related to one another, his breach by non-performance as to less than the whole, whether or not accompanied or followed by a repudiation, does not give rise to a claim for damages for total breach.

(4) In any case other than those stated in the preceding subsections, a breach by non-performance gives rise to a claim for total breach only if it so substantially impairs the value of the contract to the injured party at the time of the breach that it is just in the circumstances to allow him to recover damages based on all his remaining rights to performance.

§ 249. When Payment Other Than By Legal Tender is Sufficient

Where the payment or offer of payment of money is made a condition of an obligor's duty, payment or offer of payment in any manner current in the ordinary course of business satisfies the requirement unless the obligee demands payment in legal tender and gives any extension of time reasonably necessary to procure it.

TOPIC 3. EFFECT OF PROSPECTIVE NON-PERFORMANCE

§ 250. When a Statement or an Act Is a Repudiation

A repudiation is

(a) a statement by the obligor to the obligee indicating that the obligor will commit a breach that would of itself give the obligee a claim for damages for total breach under § 243, or

(b) a voluntary affirmative act which renders the obligor unable or apparently unable to perform without such a breach.

§251. When a Failure to Give Assurance May Be Treated as a Repudiation

(1) Where reasonable grounds arise to believe that the obligor will commit a breach by non-performance that would of itself give the obligee a claim for damages for total breach under §243, the obligee may demand adequate assurance of due performance and may, if reasonable, suspend any performance for which he has not already received the agreed exchange until he receives such assurance.

(2) The obligee may treat as a repudiation the obligor's failure to provide within a reasonable time such assurance of due performance as is adequate in the circumstances of the particular case.

§253. Effect of a Repudiation as a Breach and on Other Party's Duties

(1) Where an obligor repudiates a duty before he has committed a breach by non-performance and before he has received all of the agreed exchange for it, his repudiation alone gives rise to a claim for damages for total breach.

(2) Where performances are to be exchanged under an exchange of promises, one party's repudiation of a duty to render performance discharges the other party's remaining duties to render performance.

CHAPTER 11 IMPRACTICABILITY OF PERFORMANCE AND FRUSTRATION OF PURPOSE

§261. Discharge by Supervening Impracticability

Where, after a contract is made, a party's performance is made impracticable without his fault by the occurrence of an event the non-occurrence of which was a basic assumption on which the contract was made, his duty to render that performance is discharged, unless the language or the circumstances indicate the contrary.

Comment:

b. Basic assumption. In order for a supervening event to discharge a duty under this Section, the non-occurrence of that event must have been a "basic assumption" on which both parties made the contract (see Introductory Note to this Chapter). This is the criterion used by Uniform Commercial Code

§ 2-615(a). Its application is simple enough in the cases of the death of a person or destruction of a specific thing necessary for performance. The continued existence of the person or thing (the non-occurrence of the death or destruction) is ordinarily a basic assumption on which the contract was made, so that death or destruction effects a discharge. Its application is also simple enough in the cases of market shifts or the financial inability of one of the parties. The continuation of existing market conditions and of the financial situation of the parties are ordinarily not such assumptions, so that mere market shifts or financial inability do not usually effect discharge under the rule stated in this Section. In borderline cases this criterion is sufficiently flexible to take account of factors that bear on a just allocation of risk. The fact that the event was foreseeable, or even foreseen, does not necessarily compel a conclusion that its non-occurrence was not a basic assumption. See Comment *c* to this Section and Comment *a* to § 265.

Illustrations:

1. On June 1, A agrees to sell and B to buy goods to be delivered in October at a designated port. The port is subsequently closed by quarantine regulations during the entire month of October, no commercially reasonable substitute performance is available (see Uniform Commercial Code § 2-614(1)), and A fails to deliver the goods. A's duty to deliver the goods is discharged, and A is not liable to B for breach of contract.

2. A contracts to produce a movie for B. As B knows, A's only source of funds is a $100,000 deposit in C bank. C bank fails, and A does not produce the movie. A's duty to produce the movie is not discharged, and A is liable to B for breach of contract.

§ 262. Death or Incapacity of Person Necessary for Performance

If the existence of a particular person is necessary for the performance of a duty, his death or such incapacity as makes performance impracticable is an event the non-occurrence of which was a basic assumption on which the contract was made.

§ 263. Destruction, Deterioration or Failure to Come Into Existence of Thing Necessary for Performance

If the existence of a specific thing is necessary for the performance of a duty, its failure to come into existence, destruction, or such deterioration as makes performance impracticable is an event the non-occurrence of which was a basic assumption on which the contract was made.

Illustrations:

1. A contracts to sell and B to buy cloth. A expects to manufacture the cloth in his factory, but before he begins manufacture the factory is

destroyed by fire without his fault. Although cloth meeting the contract description is available on the market, A refuses to buy and deliver it to B. A's duty to deliver the cloth is not discharged, and A is liable to B for breach of contract.

2. The facts being otherwise as stated in Illustration 1, A contracts to sell cloth to be manufactured in the factory that is later destroyed. A's duty to deliver the cloth is discharged, and A is not liable to B for breach of contract.

§ 264. Prevention by Governmental Regulation or Order

If the performance of a duty is made impracticable by having to comply with a domestic or foreign governmental regulation or order, that regulation or order is an event the non-occurrence of which was a basic assumption on which the contract was made.

Comment:

a. Rationale. This Section, like the two that precede it, states a specific instance for the application of the rule stated in § 261. It is "a basic assumption on which the contract was made" that the law will not directly intervene to make performance impracticable when it is due. Therefore, if supervening governmental action prohibits a performance or imposes requirements that make it impracticable, the duty to render that performance is discharged, subject to the qualifications stated in § 261. The fact that it is still possible for a party to perform if he is willing to break the law and risk the consequences does not bar him from claiming discharge. The rule stated in this Section does not apply if the language or the circumstances indicate the contrary. With the trend toward greater governmental regulation, however, parties are increasingly aware of such risks, and a party may undertake a duty that is not discharged by such supervening governmental actions, as where governmental approval is required for his performance and he assumes the risk that approval will be denied.

§ 265. Discharge by Supervening Frustration

Where, after a contract is made, a party's principal purpose is substantially frustrated without his fault by the occurrence of an event the non-occurrence of which was a basic assumption on which the contract was made, his remaining duties to render performance are discharged, unless the language or the circumstances indicate the contrary.

Comment:

a. Rationale. This Section deals with the problem that arises when a change in circumstances makes one party's performance virtually worthless to the other, frustrating his purpose in making the contract. It is distinct from the problem of impracticability dealt with in the four preceding sections because there is no impediment to performance by either party. Although there has been no true failure of performance in the sense required for the application of the rule stated in § 237, the impact on the party adversely affected will be similar. The rule stated in this Section sets out the requirements for the discharge of that party's duty. First, the purpose that is frustrated must have been a principal purpose of that party in making the contract. It is not enough that he had in mind some specific object without which he would not have made the contract. The object must be so completely the basis of the contract that, as both parties understand, without it the transaction would make little sense. Second, the frustration must be substantial. It is not enough that the transaction has become less profitable for the affected party or even that he will sustain a loss. The frustration must be so severe that it is not fairly to be regarded as within the risks that he assumed under the contract. Third, the non-occurrence of the frustrating event must have been a basic assumption on which the contract was made. This involves essentially the same sorts of determinations that are involved under the general rule on impracticability. See Comments *b* and *c* to § 261. The foreseeability of the event is here, as it is there, a factor in that determination, but the mere fact that the event was foreseeable does not compel the conclusion that its non-occurrence was not such a basic assumption.

Illustrations:

1. A and B make a contract under which B is to pay A $1,000 and is to have the use of A's window on January 10 to view a parade that has been scheduled for that day. Because of the illness of an important official, the parade is cancelled. B refuses to use the window or pay the $1,000. B's duty to pay $1,000 is discharged, and B is not liable to A for breach of contract.

2. A contracts with B to print an advertisement in a souvenir program of an international yacht race, which has been scheduled by a yacht club, for a price of $10,000. The yacht club cancels the race because of the outbreak of war. A has already printed the programs, but B refuses to pay the $10,000. B's duty to pay $10,000 is discharged, and B is not liable to A for breach of contract. A may have a claim under the rule stated in § 272(1).

6. A leases a gasoline station to B. A change in traffic regulations so reduces B's business that he is unable to operate the station except at a substantial loss. B refuses to make further payments of rent. If B can still operate the station, even though at such a loss, his principal purpose of operating a gasoline station is not substantially frustrated. B's duty to pay rent is not discharged, and B is liable to A for breach of contract. The result would be the same if substantial loss were caused instead by a government regulation rationing gasoline or a termination of the franchise under which B obtained gasoline.

§ 266. Existing Impracticability or Frustration

(1) Where, at the time a contract is made, a party's performance under it is impracticable without his fault because of a fact of which he has no reason to know and the non-existence of which is a basic assumption on which the

contract is made, no duty to render that performance arises, unless the language of circumstances indicate the contrary.

(2)Where, at the time a contract is made, a party's principal purpose is substantially frustrated without his fault by a fact of which he has no reason to know and the non-existence of which is a basic assumption on which the contract is made, no duty of that party to render performance arises, unless the language or circumstances indicate the contrary.

§ 271. Impracticability as Excuse for Non-Occurrence of a Condition

Impracticability excuses the non-occurrence of a condition if the occurrence of the condition is not a material part of the agreed exchange and forfeiture would otherwise result.

CHAPTER 12 DISCHARGE BY ASSENT OR ALTERATION

TOPIC 1. THE REQUIREMENT OF CONSIDERATION

§ 273. Requirement of Consideration or a Substitute

Except as stated in §§ 274-77, an obligee's manifestation of assent to a discharge is not effective unless

(a) it is made for consideration,

(b) it is made in circumstances in which a promise would be enforceable without consideration,

(c) it has induced such action or forbearance as would make a promise enforceable.

Comment:

a. Rationale. This section states the traditional requirement of consideration or one of its substitutes in order that the obligee's assent to even a present discharge be effective. The requirement is analogous to that of consideration or some substitute in order that even a present transfer of a right by assignment be irrevocable (§ 332). Subject to some exceptions, a gratuitous discharge is not effective, just as a gratuitous promise is not enforceable and a gratuitous assignment is not irrevocable. The use of words suggesting present transfer, such as those of gift or of assignment, does not affect the result. See Illustration 1.

Illustrations:

1. A, whom B owes $1,000 for goods delivered, gives B a signed writing that states, "I hereby irrevocably give, transfer, assign and release my right to the $1,000 that you owe me." B's debt is not discharged. Compare § 284 with § 332(1)(a).

§ 279. Substituted Contract

(1) A substituted contract is a contract that is itself accepted by the obligee in satisfaction of the obligor's existing duty.

(2) The substituted contact discharges the original duty and breach of the substituted contract by the obligor does not give the obligee a right to enforce the original duty.

Comment:

a. Nature and effect of a substituted contract. A substituted contract is one that is itself accepted by the obligee in satisfaction of the original duty and thereby discharges it. A common type of substituted contract is one that contains a term that is inconsistent with a term of an earlier contract between the parties. If the parties intend the new contract to replace all of the provisions of the earlier contract, the contract is a substituted contract. If a substituted contract brings in a new party it is called a "novation" (§ 280).

Illustrations:

1. A is under a duty to deliver a tractor to B on July 1. On June 1, A offers to deliver a bulldozer to B on July 1 if B will accept his promise in satisfaction of A's duty to deliver the tractor, and B accepts. The contract is a substituted contract. A's duty to deliver the tractor is discharged. If A does not deliver the bulldozer, B can enforce the duty to deliver it but not the original duty to deliver the tractor.

2. A and B make a contract under which A promises to build on a designated spot a building, for which B promises to pay $100,000. Later, before this contract is performed, A and B make a new contract under which A is to build on the same spot a different building, for which B is to pay $200,000. The new contract is a substituted contract and the duties of A and B under the original contract are discharged.

b. Validity of substituted contract. Under the rule stated in § 273, although the discharge that results from a substituted contract is an immediate change in the legal relations between the obligor and oblige and involves no promise by the obligee, it is not effective unless it is supported by consideration or some substitute for consideration.

TOPIC 2. SUBSTITUTED PERFORMANCE, SUBSTITUTED CONTRACT, ACCORD AND ACCOUNT STATED

§ 280. Novation

A novation is a substituted contract that includes as a party one who was neither the obligor nor the obligee of the original duty.

Comment:

b. Effect of novation. A novation discharges the original duty, just as any other substituted contract does, so that breach of the new duty gives no right of action on the old duty. Most novations simply substitute a new obligor for an old obligor or, less commonly, a new obligee for an old obligee. . . .

Illustration:

1. A owes B $1,000. B promises A that he will discharge the debt immediately if C will promise B to pay B $1,000. C so promises. There is a novation under which B's and C's promises are consideration for each other and A is discharged.

§ 281. Accord and Satisfaction

(1) An accord is a contract under which an oblige promises to accept a stated performance in satisfaction of the obligor's existing duty. Performance of the accord discharges the original duty.

(2) Until performance of the accord, the original duty is suspended unless there is such a breach of the accord by the obligor as discharges the new duty of the obligee to accept the performance in satisfaction. If there is such a breach, the obligee may enforce either the original duty or any duty under the accord.

(3) Breach of the accord by the oblige does not discharge the original duty, but the obligor may maintain a suit for specific performance of the accord, in addition to any claim for damages for partial breach.

TOPIC 3. AGREEMENT OF RESCISSION, RELEASE AND CONTRACT NOT TO SUE

§ 283. Agreement of Rescission

(1) An agreement of rescission is an agreement under which each party agrees to discharge all of the other party's remaining duties of performance under an existing contract.

(2) An agreement of rescission discharges all remaining duties of performance of both parties. It is a question of interpretation whether the parties also agree to make restitution with respect to performance that has been rendered.

CHAPTER 13 JOINT AND SEVERAL PROMISORS AND PROMISEES

[NOT EXCERPTED]

CHAPTER 14 CONTRACT BENEFICIARIES

[NOT EXCERPTED]

CHAPTER 15 ASSIGNMENT AND DELEGATION

[NOT EXCERPTED]

CHAPTER 16 REMEDIES

TOPIC 1. IN GENERAL

§ 344. Purposes of Remedies

Judicial remedies under the rules stated in this Restatement serve to protect one or more of the following interests of a promisee:

(a) his "expectation interest," which is his interest in having the benefit of his bargain by being put in as good a position as he would have been in had the contract been performed,

(b) his "reliance interest," which is his interest in being reimbursed for loss caused by reliance on the contract by being put in as good a position as he would have been in had the contract not been made, or

(c) his "restitution interest," which is his interest in having restored to him any benefit that he has conferred on the other party.

§ 345. Judicial Remedies Available

The judicial remedies available for the protection of the interests stated in § 344 include a judgment or order

(a) awarding a sum of money due under the contract or as damages,

(b) requiring specific performance of a contract or enjoining its non-performance,

(c) requiring restoration of a specific thing to prevent unjust enrichment,

(d) awarding a sum of money to prevent unjust enrichment,

(e) declaring the rights of the parties, and

(f) enforcing an arbitration award.

TOPIC 2. ENFORCEMENT BY AWARD OF DAMAGES

§346. Availability of Damages

(1) The injured party has a right to damages for any breach by a party against whom the contract is enforceable unless the claim for damages has been suspended or discharged.

(2) If the breach caused no loss or if the amount of the loss is not proved under the rules stated in this Chapter, a small sum fixed without regard to the amount of loss will be awarded as nominal damages.

Comment:

b. Nominal damages. Although a breach of contract by a party against whom it is enforceable always gives rise to a claim for damages, there are instances in which the breach causes no loss. See Illustration 1. There are also instances in which loss is caused but recovery for that loss is precluded because it cannot be proved with reasonable certainty or because of one of the other limitations stated in this Chapter. See §§350-53. In all these instances the injured party will nevertheless get judgment for nominal damages, a small sum usually fixed by judicial practice in the jurisdiction in which the action is brought. Such a judgment may, in the discretion of the court, carry with it an award of court costs. Costs are generally awarded if a significant right was involved or the claimant made a good faith effort to prove damages, but not if the maintenance of the action was frivolous or in bad faith. Unless a significant right is involved, a court will not reverse and remand a case for a new trial if only nominal damages could result.

Illustration:

1. A contracts to sell to B 1,000 shares of stock in X Corporation for $10 a share to be delivered on June 1, but breaks the contract by refusing on that date to deliver the stock. B sues A for damages, but at trial it is proved that B could have purchased 1,000 shares of stock in X Corporation on the market on June 1 for $10 a share and therefore has suffered no loss. In an action by B against A, B will be awarded nominal damages.

§347. Measure of Damages in General

Subject to the limitations stated in §§350-53, the injured party has a right to damages based on his expectation interest as measured by

(a) the loss in the value to him of the other party's performance caused by its failure or deficiency, plus

(b) any other loss, including incidental or consequential loss, caused by the breach, less

(c) any cost or other loss that he has avoided by not having to perform.

Comment:

a. Expectation interest. Contract damages are ordinarily based on the injured party's expectation interest and are intended to give him the benefit of his bargain by awarding him a sum of money that will, to the extent possible, put him in as good a position as he would have been in had the contract been performed. See § 344(1)(a). In some situations the sum awarded will do this adequately as, for example, where the injured party has simply had to pay an additional amount to arrange a substitute transaction and can be adequately compensated by damages based on that amount. In other situations the sum awarded cannot adequately compensate the injured party for his disappointed expectation as, for example, where a delay in performance has caused him to miss an invaluable opportunity. The measure of damages stated in this Section is subject to the agreement of the parties, as where they provide for liquidated damages (§ 356) or exclude liability for consequential damages.

b. Loss in value. The first element that must be estimated in attempting to fix a sum that will fairly represent the expectation interest is the loss in the value to the injured party of the other party's performance that is caused by the failure of, or deficiency in, that performance. If no performance is rendered, the loss in value caused by the breach is equal to the value that the performance would have had to the injured party. See Illustrations 1 and 2. If defective or partial performance is rendered, the loss in value caused by the breach is equal to the difference between the value that the performance would have had if there had been no breach and the value of such performance as was actually rendered. In principle, this requires a determination of the values of those performances to the injured party himself and not their values to some hypothetical reasonable person or on some market. . . . They therefore depend on his own particular circumstances or those of his enterprise, unless consideration of these circumstances is precluded by the limitation of foreseeability (§ 351). Where the injured party's expected advantage consists largely or exclusively of the realization of profit, it may be possible to express this loss in value in terms of money with some assurance. In other situations, however, this is not possible and compensation for lost value may be precluded by the limitation of certainty. See § 352. In order to facilitate the estimation of loss with sufficient certainty to award damages, the injured party is sometimes given a choice between alternative bases of calculating his loss in value. The most important of these are stated in § 348. See also §§ 349 and 373.

Illustrations:

1. A contracts to publish a novel that B has written. A repudiates the contract and B is unable to get his novel published elsewhere. Subject to the limitations stated in §§ 350-53, B's damages include the loss of royalties that he would have received had the novel been published together with the value to him of the resulting enhancement of his reputation. . . .

2. A, a manufacturer, contracts to sell B, a dealer in used machinery, a used machine that B plans to resell. A repudiates and B is unable to obtain a similar machine elsewhere. Subject to the limitations stated in §§ 350-53, B's damages include the net profit that he would have made on resale of the machine.

c. Other loss. Subject to the limitations stated in §§ 350-53, the injured party is entitled to recover for all loss actually suffered. Items of loss other than loss in value of the other party's performance are often characterized as incidental or consequential. Incidental losses include costs incurred in a reasonable effort, whether successful or not, to avoid loss, as where a party pays brokerage fees in arranging or attempting to arrange a substitute transaction. See Illustration 3. Consequential losses include such items as injury to person or property resulting from defective performance. See Illustration 4. The terms used to describe the type of loss are not, however, controlling, and the general principle is that all losses, however described, are recoverable.

Illustration:

3. A contracts to employ B for $10,000 to supervise the production of A's crop, but breaks his contract by firing B at the beginning of the season. B reasonably spends $200 in fees attempting to find other suitable employment through appropriate agencies. B can recover the $200 incidental loss in addition to any other loss suffered, whether or not he succeeds in finding other employment.

d. Cost or other loss avoided. Sometimes the breach itself results in a saving of some cost that the injured party would have incurred if he had had to perform. See Illustration 5. Furthermore, the injured party is expected to take reasonable steps to avoid further loss. See § 350. Where he does this by discontinuing his own performance, he avoids incurring additional costs of performance. . . . This cost avoided is subtracted from the loss in value caused by the breach in calculating his damages. If the injured party avoids further loss by making substitute arrangements for the use of his resources that are no longer needed to perform the contract, the net profit from such arrangements is also subtracted. . . . The value to him of any salvageable materials that he has acquired for performance is also subtracted. . . . Loss avoided is subtracted only if the saving results from the injured party not having to perform rather than from some unrelated event. . . . If no cost or other loss has been avoided, however, the injured party's damages include the full amount of the loss in value with no subtraction, subject to the limitations stated in §§ 350-53. . . . The intended "donee" beneficiary of a gift promise usually suffers loss to the full extent of the value of the promised performance, since he is ordinarily not required to do anything, and so avoids no cost on breach. See § 302(1)(b).

Illustration:

5. A contracts to build a hotel for B for $500,000 and to have it ready for occupancy by May 1. B's occupancy of the hotel is delayed for a month

because of a breach by A. The cost avoided by B as a result of not having to operate the hotel during May is subtracted from the May rent lost in determining B's damages.

e. Actual loss caused by breach. The injured party is limited to damages based on his actual loss caused by the breach. If he makes an especially favorable substitute transaction, so that he sustains a smaller loss than might have been expected, his damages are reduced by the loss avoided as a result of that transaction. See Illustration 12. If he arranges a substitute transaction that he would not have been expected to do under the rules on avoidability (§ 350), his damages are similarly limited by the loss so avoided. . . . Recovery can be had only for loss that would not have occurred but for the breach. See § 346. If, after the breach, an event occurs that would have discharged the party in breach on grounds of impracticability of performance or frustration of purpose, damages are limited to the loss sustained prior to that event. . . . Compare § 254(2). The principle that a party's liability is not reduced by payments or other benefits received by the injured party from collateral sources is less compelling in the case of a breach of contract than in the case of a tort. . . . The effect of the receipt of unemployment benefits by a discharged employee will turn on the court's perception of legislative policy rather than on the rule stated in this Section. . . .

Illustration:

12. A contracts to build a house for B for $100,000, but repudiates the contract after doing part of the work and having been paid $40,000. Other builders would charge B $80,000 to finish the house, but B finds a builder in need of work who does it for $70,000. B's damages are limited to the $70,000 that he actually had to pay to finish the work less the $60,000 cost avoided or $10,000, together with damages for any loss caused by the delay. . . .

f. Lost volume. Whether a subsequent transaction is a substitute for the broken contract sometimes raises difficult questions of fact. If the injured party could and would have entered into the subsequent contract, even if the contract had not been broken, and could have had the benefit of both, he can be said to have "lost volume" and the subsequent transaction is not a substitute for the broken contract. The injured party's damages are then based on the net profit that he has lost as a result of the broken contract. Since entrepreneurs try to operate at optimum capacity, however, it is possible that an additional transaction would not have been profitable and that the injured party would not have chosen to expand his business by undertaking it had there been no breach. It is sometimes assumed that he would have done so, but the question is one of fact to be resolved according to the circumstances of each case. See Illustration 16. See also Uniform Commercial Code § 2-708(2).

Illustration:

16. A contracts to pave B's parking lot for $10,000. B repudiates the contract and A subsequently makes a contract to pave a similar parking lot for $10,000. A's business could have been expanded to do both jobs. Unless it is proved that he would not have undertaken both, A's damages are

based on the net profit he would have made on the contract with B, without regard to the subsequent transaction.

§ 348. Alternatives to Loss in Value of Performance

(1) If a breach delays the use of property and the loss in value to the injured party is not proved with reasonable certainty, he may recover damages based on the rental value of the property or on interest on the value of the property.

(2) If a breach results in defective or unfinished construction and the loss in value to the injured party is not proved with sufficient certainty, he may recover damages based on

(a) the diminution in the market price of the property caused by the breach, or

(b) the reasonable cost of completing performance or of remedying the defects if that cost is not clearly disproportionate to the probable loss in value to him.

(3) If a breach is of a promise conditioned on a fortuitous event and it is uncertain whether the event would have occurred had there been no breach, the injured party may recover damages based on the value of the conditional right at the time of breach.

Comment:

a. Reason for alternative bases. Although in principle the injured party is entitled to recover based on the loss in value to him caused by the breach, in practice he may be precluded from recovery on this basis because he cannot show the loss in value to him with sufficient certainty. See § 352. In such a case, if there is a reasonable alternative to loss in value, he may claim damages based on that alternative. This Section states the rules that have been developed for three such cases.

§ 349. Damages Based on Reliance Interest

As an alternative to the measure of damages stated in § 347, the injured party has a right to damages based on his reliance interest, including expenditures made in preparation for performance or in performance, less any loss that the party in breach can prove with reasonable certainty the injured party would have suffered had the contract been performed.

§ 350. Avoidability as a Limitation on Damages

(1) Except as stated in Subsection (2), damages are not recoverable for loss that the injured party could have avoided without undue risk, burden or humiliation.

(2) The injured party is not precluded from recovery by the rule stated in Subsection (1) to the extent that he has made reasonable but unsuccessful efforts to avoid loss.

§ 351. Unforeseeability and Related Limitations on Damages

(1) Damages are not recoverable for loss that the party in breach did not have reason to foresee as a probable result of the breach when the contract was made.

(2) Loss may be foreseeable as a probable result of a breach because it follows from the breach

(a) in the ordinary course of events, or

(b) as a result of special circumstances, beyond the ordinary course of events, that the party in breach had reason to know.

(3) A court may limit damages for foreseeable loss by excluding recovery for loss of profits, by allowing recovery only for loss incurred in reliance, or otherwise if it concludes that in the circumstances justice so requires in order to avoid disproportionate compensation.

Comment:

a. Requirement of foreseeability. A contracting party is generally expected to take account of those risks that are foreseeable at the time he makes the contract. He is not, however, liable in the event of breach for loss that he did not at the time of contracting have reason to foresee as a probable result of such a breach. The mere circumstance that some loss was foreseeable, or even that some loss of the same general kind was foreseeable, will not suffice if the loss that actually occurred was not foreseeable. It is enough, however, that the loss was foreseeable as a probable, as distinguished from a necessary, result of his breach. Furthermore, the party in breach need not have made a "tacit agreement" to be liable for the loss. Nor must he have had the loss in mind when making the contract, for the test is an objective one based on what he had reason to foresee. There is no requirement of foreseeability with respect to the injured party. In spite of these qualifications, the requirement of foreseeability is a more severe limitation of liability than is the requirement of substantial or "proximate" cause in the case of an action in tort or for breach of warranty. . . . Uniform Commercial Code § 2-715(2)(b). Although the recovery that is precluded by the limitation of foreseeability is usually based on the expectation interest and takes the form of lost profits . . . the limitation may also preclude recovery based on the reliance interest[.]

§ 352. Uncertainty as a Limitation on Damages

Damages are not recoverable for loss beyond an amount that the evidence permits to be established with reasonable certainty.

§353. Loss Due to Emotional Disturbance

Recovery for emotional disturbance will be excluded unless the breach also caused bodily harm or the contract or the breach is of such a kind that serious emotional disturbance was a particularly likely result.

Comment:

a. Emotional disturbance. Damages for emotional disturbance are not ordinarily allowed. Even if they are foreseeable, they are often particularly difficult to establish and to measure. There are, however, two exceptional situations where such damages are recoverable. In the first, the disturbance accompanies a bodily injury. In such cases the action may nearly always be regarded as one in tort, although most jurisdictions do not require the plaintiff to specify the nature of the wrong on which his action is based and award damages without classifying the wrong. . . . In the second exceptional situation, the contract or the breach is of such a kind that serious emotional disturbance was a particularly likely result. Common examples are contracts of carriers and innkeepers with passengers and guests, contracts for the carriage or proper disposition of dead bodies, and contracts for the delivery of messages concerning death. Breach of such a contract is particularly likely to cause serious emotional disturbance. Breach of other types of contracts, resulting for example in sudden impoverishment or bankruptcy, may by chance cause even more severe emotional disturbance, but, if the contract is not one where this was a particularly likely risk, there is no recovery for such disturbance.

§354. Interest as Damages

(1) If the breach consists of a failure to pay a definite sum in money or to render a performance with fixed or ascertainable monetary value, interest is recoverable from the time for performance on the amount due less all deductions to which the party in breach is entitled.

(2) In any other case, such interest may be allowed as justice requires on the amount that would have been just compensation had it been paid when performance was due.

§355. Punitive Damages

Punitive damages are not recoverable for a breach of contract unless the conduct constituting the breach is also a tort for which punitive damages are recoverable.

§ 356. Liquidated Damages and Penalties

(1) Damages for breach by either party may be liquidated in the agreement but only at an amount that is reasonable in the light of the anticipated or actual loss caused by the breach and the difficulties of proof of loss. A term fixing unreasonably large liquidated damages is unenforceable on grounds of public policy as a penalty.

(2) A term in a bond providing for an amount of money as a penalty for non-occurrence of the condition of the bond is unenforceable on grounds of public policy to the extent that the amount exceeds the loss caused by such non-occurrence.

TOPIC 3. ENFORCEMENT BY SPECIFIC PERFORMANCE AND INJUNCTION

§ 357. Availability of Specific Performance and Injunction

(1) Subject to the rules stated in §§ 359-69, specific performance of a contract duty will be granted in the discretion of the court against a party who has committed or is threatening to commit a breach of the duty.

(2) Subject to the rules stated in §§ 359-69, an injunction against breach of a contract duty will be granted in the discretion of the court against a party who has committed or is threatening to commit a breach of the duty if

(a) the duty is one of forbearance, or

(b) the duty is one to act and specific performance would be denied only for reasons that are inapplicable to an injunction.

§ 358. Form of Order and Other Relief

(1) An order of specific performance or an injunction will be so drawn as best to effectuate the purposes for which the contract was made and on such terms as justice requires. It need not be absolute in form and the performance that it requires need not be identical with that due under the contract.

(2) If specific performance or an injunction is denied as to part of the performance that is due, it may nevertheless be granted as to the remainder.

(3) In addition to specific performance or an injunction, damages and other relief may be awarded in the same proceeding and an indemnity against future harm may be required.

§ 359. Effect of Adequacy of Damages

(1) Specific performance or an injunction will not be ordered if damages would be adequate to protect the expectation interest of the injured party.

(2) The adequacy of the damage remedy for failure to render one part of the performance due does not preclude specific performance or injunction as to the contract as a whole.

(3) Specific performance or an injunction will not be refused merely because there is a remedy for breach other than damages, but such a remedy may be considered in exercising discretion under the rule stated in § 357.

Comment:

a. Bases for requirement. The underlying objective in choosing the form of relief to be granted is to select a remedy that will adequately protect the legally recognized interest of the injured party. If, as is usually the case, that interest is the expectation interest, the remedy may take the form either of damages or of specific performance or an injunction. As to the situation in which the interest to be protected is the restitution interest, see § 373.

During the development of the jurisdiction of courts of equity, it came to be recognized that equitable relief would not be granted if the award of damages at law was adequate to protect the interests of the injured party. There is, however, a tendency to liberalize the granting of equitable relief by enlarging the classes of cases in which damages are not regarded as an adequate remedy. This tendency has been encouraged by the adoption of the Uniform Commercial Code, which "seeks to further a more liberal attitude than some courts have shown in connection with the specific performance of contracts of sale." Comment 1 to Uniform Commercial Code § 2-716. In accordance with this tendency, if the adequacy of the damage remedy is uncertain, the combined effect of such other factors as uncertainty of terms (§ 362), insecurity as to the agreed exchange (§ 363) and difficulty of enforcement (§ 366) should be considered. Adequacy is to some extent relative, and the modern approach is to compare remedies to determine which is more effective in serving the ends of justice. Such a comparison will often lead to the granting of equitable relief. Doubts should be resolved in favor of the granting of specific performance or injunction.

Because the availability of equitable relief was historically viewed as a matter of jurisdiction, the parties cannot vary by agreement the requirement of inadequacy of damages, although a court may take appropriate notice of facts recited in their contract. . . .

§ 360. Factors Affecting Adequacy of Damages

In determining whether the remedy in damages would be adequate, the following circumstances are significant:

(a) the difficulty of proving damages with reasonable certainty,

(b) the difficulty of procuring a suitable substitute performance by means of money awarded as damages, and

(c) the likelihood that an award of damages could not be collected.

§ 361. Effect of Provision for Liquidated Damages

Specific performance or an injunction may be granted to enforce a duty even though there is a provision for liquidated damages for breach of that duty.

Comment:

a. Rationale. A contract provision for payment of a sum of money as damages may not afford an adequate remedy even though it is valid as one for liquidated damages and not a penalty (§ 356). Merely by providing for liquidated damages, the parties are not taken to have fixed a price to be paid for the privilege not to perform. The same uncertainty as to the loss caused that argues for the enforceability of the provision may also argue for the inadequacy of the remedy that it provides. Such a provision does not, therefore, preclude the granting of specific performance or an injunction if that relief would otherwise be granted. If the provision is unenforceable as one for a penalty, the same result follows, but because of the ineffectiveness of the clause rather than the operation of the rule here stated.

§ 362. Effect of Uncertainty of Terms

Specific performance or injunction will not be granted unless the terms of the contract are sufficiently certain to provide a basis for an appropriate order.

§ 363. Effect of Insecurity as to the Agreed Exchange

Specific performance or an injunction may be refused if a substantial part of the agreed exchange for the performance to be compelled is unperformed and its performance is not secured to the satisfaction of the court.

§ 364. Effect of Unfairness

(1) Specific performance or an injunction will be refused if such relief would be unfair because

(a) the contract was induced by mistake or by unfair practices,

(b) the relief would cause unreasonable hardship or loss to the party in breach or to third persons, or

(c) the exchange is grossly inadequate or the terms of the contract are otherwise unfair.

(2) Specific performance or an injunction will be granted in spite of a term of the agreement if denial of such relief would be unfair because it would cause unreasonable hardship or loss to the party seeking relief or to third persons.

§365. Effect of Public Policy

Specific performance or an injunction will not be granted if the act or forbearance that would be compelled or the use of compulsion is contrary to public policy.

§366. Effect of Difficulty in Enforcement or Supervision

A promise will not be specifically enforced if the character and magnitude of the performance would impose on the court burdens in enforcement or supervision that are disproportionate to the advantages to be gained from enforcement and to the harm to be suffered from its denial.

§367. Contracts for Personal Service or Supervision

(1) A promise to render personal service will not be specifically enforced.

(2) A promise to render personal service exclusively for one employer will not be enforced by an injunction against serving another if its probable result will be to compel a performance involving personal relations the enforced continuance of which is undesirable or will be to leave the employee without other reasonable means of making a living.

Comment:

a. Rationale of refusal of specific performance. A court will refuse to grant specific performance of a contract for service or supervision that is personal in nature. The refusal is based in part upon the undesirability of compelling the continuance of personal association after disputes have arisen and confidence and loyalty are gone and, in some instances, of imposing what might seem like involuntary servitude. To this extent the rule stated in Subsection (1) is an application of the more general rule under which specific performance will not be granted if the use of compulsion is contrary to public policy (§365). The refusal is also based upon the difficulty of enforcement inherent in passing judgment on the quality of performance. To this extent the rule stated in Subsection (1) is an application of the more general rule on the effect of difficulty of enforcement (§366).

§ 368. Effect of Power of Termination

(1) Specific performance or an injunction will not be granted against a party who can substantially nullify the effect of the order by exercising a power of termination or avoidance.

(2) Specific performance or an injunction will not be denied merely because the party seeking relief has a power to terminate or avoid his duty unless the power could be used, in spite of the order, to deprive the other party of reasonable security for the agreed exchange for his performance.

§ 369. Effect of Breach by Party Seeking Relief

Specific performance or an injunction may be granted in spite of a breach by the party seeking relief, unless the breach is serious enough to discharge the other party's remaining duties of performance.

TOPIC 4. RESTITUTION

§ 370. Requirement That Benefit Be Conferred

A party is entitled to restitution under the rules stated in this Restatement only to the extent that he has conferred a benefit on the other party by way of part performance or reliance.

§ 371. Measure of Restitution Interest

If a sum of money is awarded to protect a party's restitution interest, it may as justice requires be measured by either

(a) the reasonable value to the other party of what he received in terms of what it would have cost him to obtain it from a person in the claimant's position, or

(b) the extent to which the other party's property has been increased in value or his other interests advanced.

§ 372. Specific Restitution

(1) Specific restitution will be granted to a party who is entitled to restitution, except that:

(a) specific restitution based on a breach by the other party under the rule stated in § 373 may be refused in the discretion of the court if it would unduly interfere with the certainty of title to land or otherwise cause injustice, and

(b) specific restitution in favor of the party in breach under the rule stated in §374 will not be granted.

(2) A decree of specific restitution may be made conditional on return of or compensation for anything that the party claiming restitution has received.

(3) If specific restitution, with or without a sum of money, will be substantially as effective as restitution in money in putting the party claiming restitution in the position he was in before rendering any performance, the other party can discharge his duty by tendering such restitution before suit is brought and keeping his tender good.

§373. Restitution When Other Party Is in Breach

(1) Subject to the rule stated in Subsection (2), on a breach by non-performance that gives rise to a claim for damages for total breach or on a repudiation, the injured party is entitled to restitution for any benefit that he has conferred on the other party by way of part performance or reliance.

(2) The injured party has no right to restitution if he has performed all of his duties under the contract and no performance by the other party remains due other than payment of a definite sum of money for that performance.

§374. Restitution in Favor of Party in Breach

(1) Subject to the rule stated in Subsection (2), if a party justifiably refuses to perform on the ground that his remaining duties of performance have been discharged by the other party's breach, the party in breach is entitled to restitution for any benefit that he has conferred by way of part performance or reliance in excess of the loss that he has caused by his own breach.

(2) To the extent that, under the manifested assent of the parties, a party's performance is to be retained in the case of breach, that party is not entitled to restitution if the value of the performance as liquidated damages is reasonable in the light of the anticipated or actual loss caused by the breach and the difficulties of proof of loss.

§375. Restitution When Contract Is Within Statute of Frauds

A party who would otherwise have a claim in restitution under a contract is not barred from restitution for the reason that the contract is unenforceable by him because of the Statute of Frauds unless the Statute provides otherwise or its purpose would be frustrated by allowing restitution.

Comment:

a. Restitution generally available. Parties to a contract that is unenforceable under the Statute of Frauds frequently act in reliance on it before discovering that it is unenforceable. A party may, for example, render services under the contract or may make improvements on land that is the subject of the contract. The rule stated in this Section allows restitution in such cases. . . . If the party claiming restitution is in breach, the right to restitution is subject to the rule stated in § 374. If the other party is in breach it is subject to the rule stated in § 373. Since allowing restitution does not amount to enforcement of the contract, it ordinarily does not contravene the policy behind the Statute. Restitution will not be allowed, however, if the Statute so provides or if restitution would frustrate the purpose of the Statute. However, the mere fact that the particular wording of the Statute makes the contract "void" is not controlling in this respect.

§ 376. Restitution When Contract Is Voidable

A party who has avoided a contract on the ground of lack of capacity, mistake, misrepresentation, duress, undue influence or abuse of a fiduciary relation is entitled to restitution for any benefit that he has conferred on the other party by way of part performance or reliance.

§ 377. Restitution in Cases of Impracticability, Frustration, Non-Occurrence of Condition or Disclaimer by Beneficiary

A party whose duty of performance does not arise or is discharged as a result of impracticability of performance, frustration of purpose, non-occurrence of a condition or disclaimer by a beneficiary is entitled to restitution for any benefit that he has conferred on the other party by way of part performance or reliance.

Uniform Commercial Code
Selected Materials

UNIFORM COMMERCIAL CODE ARTICLE 1
Selected Materials

The American Law Institute and
The National Conference of Commissioners on Uniform State Laws

TABLE OF CONTENTS

UNIFORM COMMERCIAL CODE—ARTICLE 1

SELECTED SECTIONS

PART 1. GENERAL PROVISIONS

§ 1-101. Short Titles.

(a) This [Act] may be cited as the Uniform Commercial Code.

(b) This article may be cited as Uniform Commercial Code—General Provisions.

§ 1-102. Scope of Article.

This article applies to a transaction to the extent that it is governed by another article of [the Uniform Commercial Code].

§ 1-103. Construction of [Uniform Commercial Code] to Promote Its Purposes and Policies; Applicability of Supplemental Principles of Law.

(a) [The Uniform Commercial Code] must be liberally construed and applied to promote its underlying purposes and policies, which are:

(1) to simplify, clarify and modernize the law governing commercial transactions;

(2) to permit the continued expansion of commercial practices through custom, usage, and agreement of the parties; and

(3) to make uniform the law among the various jurisdictions.

(b) Unless displaced by the particular provisions of [the Uniform Commercial Code], the principles of law and equity, including the law merchant and the law relative to capacity to contract, principal and agent, estoppels, fraud, misrepresentation, duress, coercion, mistake, bankruptcy, and other validating or invalidating cause supplement its provisions.

§ 1-107. Section Captions.

Section captions are part of [the Uniform Commercial Code].

PART 2. GENERAL DEFINITIONS AND PRINCIPLES OF INTERPRETATION

§ 1-201. General Definitions.

(a) Unless the context otherwise requires, words or phrases defined in this section, or in the additional definitions contained in other articles of [the Uniform Commercial Code] that apply to particular articles or parts thereof, have the meanings stated.

(b) Subject to definitions contained in other articles of [the Uniform Commercial Code] that apply to particular articles or parts thereof:

(1) "Action", in the sense of a judicial proceeding, includes recoupment, counterclaim, set-off, suit in equity, and any other proceeding in which rights are determined.

(2) "Aggrieved party" means a party entitled to pursue a remedy.

(3) "Agreement", as distinguished from "contract", means the bargain of the parties in fact, as found in their language or inferred from other circumstances, including course of performance, course of dealing, or usage of trade as provided in Section 1-303.

(8) "Burden of establishing" a fact means the burden of persuading the trier of fact that the existence of the fact is more probable than its nonexistence.

(9) "Buyer in ordinary course of business" means a person that buys goods in good faith, without knowledge that the sale violates the rights of another person in the goods, and in the ordinary course from a person, other than a pawnbroker, in the business of selling goods of that kind. A person buys goods in the ordinary course if the sale to the person comports with the usual or customary practices in the kind of business in which the seller is engaged or with the seller's own usual or customary practices. A person that sells oil, gas, or other minerals at the wellhead or minehead is a person in the business of selling goods of that kind. A buyer in ordinary course of business may buy for cash, by exchange of other property, or on secured or unsecured credit, and may acquire goods or documents of title under a preexisting contract for sale. Only a buyer that takes possession of the goods or has a right to recover the goods from the seller under Article 2 may be a buyer in ordinary course of business. "Buyer in ordinary course of business" does not include a person that acquires goods in a transfer in bulk or as security for or in total or partial satisfaction of a money debt.

(10) "Conspicuous", with reference to a term, means so written, displayed, or presented that a reasonable person against which it is to operate ought to have noticed it. Whether a term is "conspicuous" or not is a decision for the court. Conspicuous terms include the following:

(A) a heading in capitals equal to or greater in size than the surrounding text, or in contrasting type, font, or color to the surrounding text of the same or lesser size; and

(B) language in the body of a record or display in larger type than the surrounding text, or in contrasting type, font, or color to the surrounding text of the same size, or set off from surrounding text of the same size by symbols or other marks that call attention to the language.

(11) "Consumer" means an individual who enters into a transaction primarily for personal, family, or household purposes.

(12) "Contract", as distinguished from "agreement", means the total legal obligation that results from the parties' agreement as determined by [the Uniform Commercial Code] as supplemented by any other applicable laws.

(14) "Defendant" includes a person in the position of defendant in a counterclaim, cross-claim, or third-party claim.

(17) "Fault" means a default, breach, or wrongful act or omission.

(18) "Fungible goods" means:

(A) goods of which any unit, by nature or usage of trade, is the equivalent of any other like unit; or

(B) goods that by agreement are treated as equivalent.

(20) "Good faith[]" ... means honesty in fact and the observance of reasonable commercial standards of fair dealing.

(24) "Money" means a medium of exchange currently authorized or adopted by a domestic or foreign government. The term includes a monetary unit of account established by an intergovernmental organization or by agreement between two or more countries.

(25) "Organization" means a person other than an individual.

(26) "Party", as distinguished from "third party", means a person that has engaged in a transaction or made an agreement subject to [the Uniform Commercial Code].

(27) "Person" means an individual, corporation, business trust, estate, trust, partnership, limited liability company, association, joint venture, government, governmental subdivision, agency, or instrumentality, public corporation, or any other legal or commercial entity.

(28) "Present value" means the amount as of a date certain of one or more sums payable in the future, discounted to the date certain by use of either an interest rate specified by the parties if that rate is not manifestly unreasonable at the time the transaction is entered into or, if an interest rate is not so specified, a commercially reasonable rate that takes into account the facts and circumstances at the time the transaction is entered into.

(29) "Purchase" means taking by sale, lease, discount, negotiation, mortgage, pledge, lien, security interest, issue or reissue, gift, or any other voluntary transaction creating an interest in property.

(30) "Purchaser" means a person that takes by purchase.

(31) "Record" means information that is inscribed on a tangible medium or that is stored in an electronic or other medium and is retrievable in perceivable form.

(32) ''Remedy'' means any remedial right to which an aggrieved party is entitled with or without resort to a tribunal.

(33) ''Representative'' means a person empowered to act for another, including an agent, an officer of a corporation or association, and a trustee, executor, or administrator of an estate.

(34) ''Right'' includes remedy.

(36) ''Send'' in connection with a writing, record, or notice means:

(A) to deposit in the mail or deliver for transmission by any other usual means of communication with postage or cost of transmission provided for and properly addressed and, in the case of an instrument, to an address specified thereon or otherwise agreed, or if there be none to any address reasonable under the circumstances; or

(B) in any other way to cause to be received any record or notice within the time it would have arrived if properly sent.

(37) ''Signed'' includes using any symbol executed or adopted with present intention to adopt or accept a writing.

(38) ''State'' means a State of the United States, the District of Columbia, Puerto Rico, the United States Virgin Islands, or any territory or insular possession subject to the jurisdiction of the United States.

(39) ''Surety'' includes a guarantor or other secondary obligor.

(40) ''Term'' means a portion of an agreement that relates to a particular matter.

(41) ''Unauthorized signature'' means a signature made without actual, implied, or apparent authority. The term includes a forgery.

(43) ''Writing'' includes printing, typewriting, or any other intentional reduction to tangible form. ''Written'' has a corresponding meaning.

Official Comment:

(20). ''Good faith.'' . . . [T]he definition of ''good faith'' in this section requires not only honesty in fact but also ''observance of reasonable commercial standards of fair dealing.'' Although ''fair dealing'' is a broad term that must be defined in context, it is clear that it is concerned with the fairness of conduct rather than the care with which an act is performed. This is an entirely different concept than whether a party exercised ordinary care in conducting a transaction. Both concepts are to be determined in the light of reasonable commercial standards, but those standards in each case are directed to different aspects of commercial conduct.

. . .

(37). ''Signed.'' This provision refers only to writings, because the term ''signed,'' as used in some articles, refers only to writings. This provision also makes it clear that, as the term ''signed'' is used in the Uniform Commercial Code, a complete signature is not necessary. The symbol may be printed, stamped or written; it may be by initials or by thumbprint. It may be on any part of the document and in appropriate cases may be found in a billhead or letterhead. No catalog of possible situations can be complete and the court must use common sense and commercial experience in passing upon these matters. The question always is whether the symbol was executed or adopted by the party with present intention to adopt or accept the writing.

§ 1-202. Notice; Knowledge.

(a) Subject to subsection (f), a person has "notice" of a fact if the person:

(1) has actual knowledge of it;

(2) has received a notice or notification of it; or

(3) from all the facts and circumstances known to the person at the time in question, has reason to know that it exists.

(b) "Knowledge" means actual knowledge. "Knows" has a corresponding meaning.

(c) "Discover", "learn", or words of similar import refer to knowledge rather than to reason to know.

(d) A person "notifies" or "gives" a notice or notification to another person by taking such steps as may be reasonably required to inform the other person in ordinary course, whether or not the other person actually comes to know of it.

(e) Subject to subsection (f), a person "receives" a notice or notification when:

(1) it comes to that person's attention; or

(2) it is duly delivered in a form reasonable under the circumstances at the place of business through which the contract was made or at another location held out by that person as the place for receipt of such communications.

(f) Notice, knowledge, or a notice or notification received by an organization is effective for a particular transaction from the time it is brought to the attention of the individual conducting that transaction and, in any event, from the time it would have been brought to the individual's attention if the organization had exercised due diligence. An organization exercises due diligence if it maintains reasonable routines for communicating significant information to the person conducting the transaction and there is reasonable compliance with the routines. Due diligence does not require an individual acting for the organization to communicate information unless the communication is part of the individual's regular duties or the individual has reason to know of the transaction and that the transaction would be materially affected by the information.

§ 1-205. Reasonable Time; Seasonableness.

(a) Whether a time for taking an action required by [the Uniform Commercial Code] is reasonable depends on the nature, purpose, and circumstances of the action.

(b) An action is taken seasonably if it is taken at or within the time agreed, or, if no time is agreed, at or within a reasonable time.

PART 3. TERRITORIAL APPLICABILITY AND GENERAL RULES

§ 1-301. Territorial Applicability; Parties' Power to Choose Applicable Law.

(a) Except as otherwise provided in this section, when a transaction bears a reasonable relation to this state and also to another state or nation the parties may agree that the law either of this state or of such other state or nation shall govern their rights and duties.

(b) In the absence of an agreement effective under subsection (a), and except as provided in subsection (c), [the Uniform Commercial Code] applies to transactions bearing an appropriate relation to this state.

§ 1-302. Variation by Agreement.

(a) Except as otherwise provided in subsection (b) or elsewhere in [the Uniform Commercial Code], the effect of provisions of [the Uniform Commercial Code] may be varied by agreement.

(b) The obligations of good faith, diligence, reasonableness, and care prescribed by [the Uniform Commercial Code] may not be disclaimed by agreement. The parties, by agreement, may determine the standards by which the performance of those obligations is to be measured if those standards are not manifestly unreasonable. Whenever [the Uniform Commercial Code] requires an action to be taken within a reasonable time, a time that is not manifestly unreasonable may be fixed by agreement.

(c) The presence in certain provisions of [the Uniform Commercial Code] of the phrase "unless otherwise agreed", or words of similar import, does not imply that the effect of other provisions may not be varied by agreement under this section.

§ 1-303. Course of Performance, Course of Dealing, and Usage of Trade.

(a) A "course of performance" is a sequence of conduct between the parties to a particular transaction that exists if:

(1) the agreement of the parties with respect to the transaction involves repeated occasions for performance by a party; and

(2) the other party, with knowledge of the nature of the performance and opportunity for objection to it, accepts the performance or acquiesces in it without objection.

(b) A "course of dealing" is a sequence of conduct concerning previous transactions between the parties to a particular transaction that is fairly to be regarded as establishing a common basis of understanding for interpreting their expressions and other conduct.

(c) A "usage of trade" is any practice or method of dealing having such regularity of observance in a place, vocation, or trade as to justify an expectation that it will be observed with respect to the transaction in question. The existence and scope of such a usage must be proved as facts. If it is established that such a usage is embodied in a trade code or similar record, the interpretation of the record is a question of law.

(d) A course of performance or course of dealing between the parties or usage of trade in the vocation or trade in which they are engaged or of which they are or should be aware is relevant in ascertaining the meaning of the parties' agreement, may give particular meaning to specific terms of the agreement, and may supplement or qualify the terms of the agreement. A usage of trade applicable in the place in which part of the performance under the agreement is to occur may be so utilized as to that part of the performance.

(e) Except as otherwise provided in subsection (f), the express terms of an agreement and any applicable course of performance, course of dealing, or usage of trade must be construed whenever reasonable as consistent with each other. If such a construction is unreasonable:

(1) express terms prevail over course of performance, course of dealing, and usage of trade;

(2) course of performance prevails over course of dealing and usage of trade; and

(3) course of dealing prevails over usage of trade.

(f) Subject to Section 2-209, a course of performance is relevant to show a waiver or modification of any term inconsistent with the course of performance.

(g) Evidence of a relevant usage of trade offered by one party is not admissible unless that party has given the other party notice that the court finds sufficient to prevent unfair surprise to the other party.

§ 1-304. Obligation of Good Faith.

Every contract or duty within [the Uniform Commercial Code] imposes an obligation of good faith on its performance and enforcement.

§ 1-305. Remedies to Be Liberally Administered.

(a) The remedies provided by [the Uniform Commercial Code] must be liberally administered to the end that the aggrieved party may be put in as good a position as if the other party had fully performed but neither consequential or special damages nor penal damages may be had except as specifically provided in [the Uniform Commercial Code] or by other rule of law.

(b) Any right or obligation declared by [the Uniform Commercial Code] is enforceable by action unless the provision declaring it specifies a different and limited effect.

UNIFORM COMMERCIAL CODE ARTICLE 2
Selected Materials

The American Law Institute and The National Conference of Commissioners on Uniform State Laws (Copyright 2012)

PART 1. SHORT TITLE, GENERAL CONSTRUCTION AND SUBJECT MATTER

§ 2-101. Short Title.
§ 2-102. Scope; Certain Security and Other Transactions Excluded from This Article.
§ 2-103. Definitions and Index of Definitions.
§ 2-104. Definitions: "Merchant"; "Between Merchants".
§ 2-105. Definitions: Transferability; "Goods"; "Future" Goods.
§ 2-106. Definitions: "Contract"; "Agreement"; "Contract for Sale"; "Sale"; "Present Sale"; "Conforming" to Contract; "Termination"; "Cancellation".

PART 2. FORM, FORMATION AND READJUSTMENT OF CONTRACT

§ 2-201. Formal Requirements; Statute of Frauds.
§ 2-202. Final Written Expression: Parol or Extrinsic Evidence.
§ 2-203. Seals Inoperative.
§ 2-204. Formation in General.
§ 2-205. Firm Offers.
§ 2-206. Offer and Acceptance in Formation of Contract.
§ 2-207. Additional Terms in Acceptance or Confirmation.
§ 2-208. Course of Performance or Practical Construction.
§ 2-209. Modification, Rescission and Waiver.

PART 3. GENERAL OBLIGATION AND CONSTRUCTION OF CONTRACT

§ 2-301. General Obligations of Parties.
§ 2-302. Unconscionable Contract or Clause.
§ 2-305. Open Price Term.
§ 2-306. Output, Requirements and Exclusive Dealings.
§ 2-308. Absence of Specified Place for Delivery.
§ 2-309. Absence of Specific Time Provisions; Notice of Termination.
§ 2-310. Open Time for Payment or Running of Credit[.]

PART 4. TITLE, CREDITORS AND GOOD FAITH PURCHASERS

[NOT EXCERPTED]

PART 5. PERFORMANCE

PART 6. BREACH, REPUDIATION, AND EXCUSE

PART 7. REMEDIES

§ 2-716. Buyer's Right to Specific Performance or Replevin.
§ 2-718. Liquidation or Limitation of Damages; Deposits.
§ 2-719. Contractual Modification or Limitation of Remedy.
§ 2-723. Proof of Market Price; Time and Place.
§ 2-724. Admissibility of Market Quotations.
§ 2-725. Statute of Limitations in Contracts for Sale.

UNIFORM COMMERCIAL CODE—ARTICLE 2

SELECTED SECTIONS

PART 1. SHORT TITLE, GENERAL CONSTRUCTION AND SUBJECT MATTER

§2-101. Short Title.

This Article shall be known and may be cited as Uniform Commercial Code—Sales.

Official Comment:

. . . The arrangement of the present Article is in terms of contract for sale and the various steps in its performance.

§2-102. Scope; Certain Security and Other Transactions Excluded from This Article.

Unless the context otherwise requires, this Article applies to transactions in goods; it does not apply to any transaction which although in the form of an unconditional contract to sell or present sale is intended to operate only as a security transaction nor does this Article impair or repeal any statute regulating sales to consumers, farmers or other specified classes of buyers.

§2-103. Definitions and Index of Definitions.

(1) In this article unless the context otherwise requires:

(a) "Buyer" means a person that buys or contracts to buy goods.

(b) "Good faith" in the case of a merchant means honesty in fact and the observance of reasonable commercial standards of fair dealing in the trade. [Reserved]

Legislative Note: The definition of "good faith" should not be adopted if the jurisdiction has enacted this definition as part of Article 1.

(c) "Receipt" of goods means taking physical possession of them.

(d) "Seller" means a person who sells or contracts to sell goods.

(2) Other definitions applying to this Article or to specified Parts thereof, and the sections in which they appear are:

"Acceptance". Section 2-606.

"Between merchants". Section 2-104.

"Contract for sale". Section 2-106.

"Cover". Section 2-712.

"Future goods". Section 2-105.
"Goods". Section 2-105.
"Identification". Section 2-501.
"Installment contract". Section 2-612.
"Merchant". Section 2-104.
"Person in position of seller". Section 2-707.
"Present sale". Section 2-106.
"Sale". Section 2-106.
"Sale on approval". Section 2-326.
"Sale or return". Section 2-326.
"Termination". Section 2-106.

. . .

(4) In addition Article 1 contains general definitions and principles of construction and interpretation applicable throughout this Article.

§ 2-104. Definitions: "Merchant"; "Between Merchants"[.]

(1) "Merchant" means a person that deals in goods of the kind or otherwise by his occupation holds himself out as having knowledge or skill peculiar to the practices or goods involved in the transaction or to whom such knowledge or skill may be attributed by his employment of an agent or broker or other intermediary who by his occupation holds himself out as having such knowledge or skill.

. . .

(3) "Between merchants" means in any transaction with respect to which both parties are chargeable with the knowledge or skill of merchants.

Official Comment:

1. This Article assumes that transactions between professionals in a given field require special and clear rules which may not apply to a casual or inexperienced seller or buyer. . . . This section lays the foundation of this policy by defining those who are to be regarded as professionals or "merchants" and by stating when a transaction is deemed to be "between merchants".
2. . . . The special provisions as to merchants appear only in this Article and they are of three kinds. Section 2-201(2), 2-205, 2-207 and 2-209 dealing with the statute of frauds, firm offers, confirmatory memoranda and modification rest on normal business practices which are or ought to be typical of and familiar to any person in business. For purposes of these sections almost every person in business would, therefore, be deemed to be a "merchant" under the language "who . . . by his occupation holds himself out as having knowledge or skill peculiar to the practices . . . involved in the transaction . . ." since the practices involved in the transaction are non-specialized business practices such as answering mail. . . . But even these sections only apply to a merchant in his mercantile capacity: a lawyer or bank president buying fishing tackle for his own use is not a merchant.

On the other hand, in Section 2-314 on the warranty of merchantability, such warranty is implied only "if the seller is a merchant with respect to goods of that kind."

A third group of sections includes 2-103(1)(b), which provides that in the case of a merchant "good faith" includes observance of reasonable commercial standards of fair dealing in the trade. . . . This group of sections applies to persons who are merchants under either the "practices" or the "goods" aspect of the definition of merchant.

§ 2-105. Definitions: Transferability; "Goods"; "Future" Goods[.]

(1) "Goods" means all things (including specially manufactured goods) which are movable at the time of identification to the contract for sale other than the money in which the price is to be paid, investment securities (Article 8) and things in action. "Goods" also includes the unborn young of animals and growing crops and other identified things attached to realty as described in the section on goods to be severed from realty (Section 2-107).

(2) Goods must be both existing and identified before any interest in them can pass. Goods which are not both existing and identified are "future" goods. A purported present sale of future goods or of any interest therein operates as a contract to sell.

(3) There may be a sale of a part interest in existing identified goods.

. . .

Official Comment:

1. . . . Goods is intended to cover the sale of money when money is being treated as a commodity but not to include it when money is the medium of payment.

§ 2-106. Definitions: "Contract"; "Agreement"; "Contract for Sale"; "Sale"; "Present Sale"; "Conforming" to Contract; "Termination"; "Cancellation".

(1) In this Article unless the context otherwise requires "contract" and "agreement" are limited to those relating to the present or future sale of goods. "Contract for sale" includes both a present sale of goods and a contract to sell goods at a future time. A "sale" consists in the passing of title from the seller to the buyer for a price[.] A "present sale" means a sale which is accomplished by the making of the contract.

(2) Goods or conduct including any part of a performance are "conforming" or conform to the contract when they are in accordance with the obligations under the contract.

(3) "Termination" occurs when either party pursuant to a power created by agreement or law puts an end to the contract otherwise than for its breach.

On "termination" all obligations which are still executory on both sides are discharged but any right based on prior breach or performance survives.

(4) "Cancellation" occurs when either party puts an end to the contract for breach by the other and its effect is the same as that of "termination" except that the cancelling party also retains any remedy for breach of the whole contract or any unperformed balance.

PART 2. FORM, FORMATION AND READJUSTMENT OF CONTRACT

§ 2-201. Formal Requirements; Statute of Frauds.

(1) Except as otherwise provided in this section a contract for the sale of goods for the price of $500[4] or more is not enforceable by way of action or defense unless there is some writing to indicate that a contract for sale has been made between the parties and signed by the party against whom enforcement is sought or by his authorized agent or broker. A writing is not insufficient because it omits or incorrectly states a term agreed upon, but the contract is not enforceable under this paragraph beyond the quantity of goods shown in such writing.

(2) Between merchants if within a reasonable time a writing in confirmation of the contract and sufficient against the sender is received and the party receiving it has reason to know its contents, it satisfies the requirements of subsection (1) against such party unless written notice of objection to its contents is given within 10 days after it is received.

(3) A contract which does not satisfy the requirements of subsection (1) but which is valid in other respects is enforceable:

(a) if the goods are to be specially manufactured for the buyer and are not suitable for sale to others in the ordinary course of the seller's business and the seller, before notice of repudiation is received and under circumstances which reasonably indicate that the goods are for the buyer, has made either a substantial beginning of their manufacture or commitments for their procurement; or

(b) if the party against whom enforcement is sought admits in his pleading, testimony or otherwise in court that a contract for sale was made, but the contract is not enforceable under this paragraph beyond the quantity of goods admitted; or

(c) with respect to goods for which payment has been made and accepted or which have been received and accepted (Sec. 2-606).

4. Some jurisdictions have increased the amount to $5,000.

Official Comment:

1. The required writing need not contain all of the material terms of the contract, and such material terms as are stated need not be precisely stated. All that is required is that the writing afford a basis for believing that the offered oral evidence rests on a real transaction. It may be written in lead pencil on a scratch pad. It need not indicate which party is the buyer and which party is the seller. The only term which must appear is the quantity term which need not be accurately stated but recovery is limited to the amount stated. The price, time and place of payment or delivery, the general quality of the goods, or any particular warranties may all be omitted

Special emphasis must be placed on the permissibility of omitting the price term in view of the insistence of some courts on the express inclusion of this term even where the parties have contracted on the basis of a published price list. In many valid contracts for sale the parties do not mention the price in express terms, the buyer being bound to pay and the seller to accept a reasonable price which the trier of the fact may well be trusted to determine. Again, frequently the price is not mentioned since the parties have based their agreement on a price list or catalogue known to both of them and this list serves as an efficient safeguard against perjury. Finally, "market" prices and valuations that are current in the vicinity constitute a similar check. Thus if the price is not stated in the memorandum it can normally be supplied without danger of fraud. Of course if the "price" consists of goods rather than money the quantity of goods must be stated.

Only three definite and invariable requirements as to the memorandum are made by this subsection. First, it must evidence a contract for the sale of goods; second, it must be "signed"; a word which includes any authentication which identifies the party to be charged; and third, it must specify a quantity.

. . .

4. Failure to satisfy the requirements of this section does not render the contract void for all purposes, but merely prevents it from being judicially enforced in favor of a party to the contract. For example, a buyer who takes possession of goods as provided in an oral contract which the seller has not meanwhile repudiated, is not a trespasser. Nor would the Statute of Frauds provisions of this section be a defense to a third person who wrongfully induces a party to refuse to perform an oral contract, even though the injured party cannot maintain an action for damages against the party so refusing to perform.

. . .

6. It is not necessary that the writing be delivered to anybody. It need not be signed or authenticated by both parties, but it is, of course, not sufficient against one who has not signed it. Prior to a dispute, no one can determine which party's signing of the memorandum may be necessary, but from the time of contracting each party should be aware that it is signing by the other which is important.

§ 2-202. Final Written Expression: Parol or Extrinsic Evidence.

Terms with respect to which the confirmatory memoranda of the parties agree or which are otherwise set forth in a writing intended by the parties as a final expression of their agreement with respect to such terms as are included therein may not be contradicted by evidence of any prior agreement or of a contemporaneous oral agreement but may be explained or supplemented

(a) by course of performance, course of dealing, or usage of trade (Section 1-303); and

(b) by evidence of consistent additional terms unless the court finds the writing to have been intended also as a complete and exclusive statement of the terms of the agreement.

Official Comment:

1. This section definitely rejects:

(a) Any assumption that because a writing has been worked out which is final on some matters, it is to be taken as including all the matters agreed upon;

(b) The premise that the language used has the meaning attributable to such language by rules of construction existing in the law rather than the meaning which arises out of the commercial context in which it was used; and

(c) The requirement that a condition precedent to the admissibility of the type of evidence specified in paragraph (a) is an original determination by the court that the language used is ambiguous.

2. Paragraph (a) makes admissible evidence of course of dealing, usage of trade and course of performance to explain or supplement the terms of any writing stating the agreement of the parties in order that the true understanding of the parties as to the agreement may be reached. Such writings are to be read on the assumption that the course of prior dealings between the parties and the usages of trade were taken for granted when the document was phrased. Unless carefully negated they have become an element of the meaning of the words used. Similarly, the course of actual performance by the parties is considered the best indication of what they intended the writing to mean.

3. Under paragraph (b) consistent additional terms, not reduced to writing, may be proved unless the court finds that the writing was intended by both parties as a complete and exclusive statement of all the terms. If the additional terms are such that, if agreed upon, they would certainly have been included in the document in the view of the court, then evidence of their alleged making must be kept from the trier of fact.

§ 2-203. Seals Inoperative.

The affixing of a seal to a writing evidencing a contract for sale or an offer to buy or sell goods does not constitute the writing a sealed instrument and the law with respect to sealed instruments does not apply to such a contract or offer.

§ 2-204. Formation in General.

(1) A contract for sale of goods may be made in any manner sufficient to show agreement, including conduct by both parties which recognizes the existence of such a contract.

(2) An agreement sufficient to constitute a contract for sale may be found even though the moment of its making is undetermined.

(3) Even though one or more terms are left open, a contract for sale does not fail for indefiniteness if the parties have intended to make a contract and there is a reasonably certain basis for giving an appropriate remedy.

§ 2-205. Firm Offers.

An offer by a merchant to buy or sell goods in a signed writing which by its terms gives assurance that it will be held open is not revocable, for lack of consideration, during the time stated or if no time is stated for a reasonable time, but in no event may such period of irrevocability exceed three months; but any such term of assurance on a form supplied by the offeree must be separately signed by the offeror.

§ 2-206. Offer and Acceptance in Formation of Contract.

(1) Unless otherwise unambiguously indicated by the language or circumstances

(a) an offer to make a contract shall be construed as inviting acceptance in any manner and by any medium reasonable in the circumstances;

(b) an order or other offer to buy goods for prompt or current shipment shall be construed as inviting acceptance either by a prompt promise to ship or by the prompt or current shipment of conforming or non-conforming goods, but such a shipment of non-conforming goods does not constitute an acceptance if the seller seasonably notifies the buyer that the shipment is offered only as an accommodation to the buyer.

(2) Where the beginning of a requested performance is a reasonable mode of acceptance an offeror who is not notified of acceptance within a reasonable time may treat the offer as having lapsed before acceptance.

Official Comment:

Purposes of Changes: To make it clear that:

1. Any reasonable manner of acceptance is intended to be regarded as available unless the offeror has made quite clear that it will not be acceptable. Former technical rules as to acceptance, such as requiring that telegraphic offers be accepted by telegraphed acceptance, etc., are rejected and a criterion that the acceptance be "in any manner and by any medium reasonable under the circumstances," is substituted. This section is intended to remain flexible and its applicability to be enlarged as new media of communication develop or as the more time-saving present day media come into general use.

3. The beginning of performance by an offeree can be effective as acceptance so as to bind the offeror only if followed within a reasonable time by notice to the offeror. Such a beginning of performance must unambiguously express the offeree's intention to engage himself. For the protection of both parties it is essential that notice follow in due course to constitute acceptance. Nothing in this section however bars the possibility that under the common law performance begun may have an intermediate effect of temporarily barring revocation of the offer, or at the offeror's option, final effect in constituting acceptance.

§ 2-207. Additional Terms in Acceptance or Confirmation.

(1) A definite and seasonable expression of acceptance or a written confirmation which is sent within a reasonable time operates as an acceptance even though it states terms additional to or different from those offered or agreed upon, unless acceptance is expressly made conditional on assent to the additional or different terms.

(2) The additional terms are to be construed as proposals for addition to the contract. Between merchants such terms become part of the contract unless:

(a) the offer expressly limits acceptance to the terms of the offer;

(b) they materially alter it; or

(c) notification of objection to them has already been given or is given within a reasonable time after notice of them is received.

(3) Conduct by both parties which recognizes the existence of a contract is sufficient to establish a contract for sale although the writings of the parties do not otherwise establish a contract. In such case the terms of the particular contract consist of those terms on which the writings of the parties agree, together with any supplementary terms incorporated under any other provisions of this Act.

Official Comment:

Purposes of Changes:

1. This section is intended to deal with two typical situations. The one is the written confirmation, where an agreement has been reached either orally or by

informal correspondence between the parties and is followed by one or both of the parties sending formal memoranda embodying the terms so far as agreed upon and adding terms not discussed. The other situation is offer and acceptance, in which a wire or letter expressed and intended as an acceptance or the closing of an agreement adds further minor suggestions or proposals such as "ship by Tuesday," "rush," "ship draft against bill of lading inspection allowed," or the like. A frequent example of the second situation is the exchange of printed purchase order and acceptance (sometimes called "acknowledgment") forms. Because the forms are oriented to the thinking of the respective drafting parties, the terms contained in them often do not correspond. Often the seller's form contains terms different from or additional to those set forth in the buyer's form. Nevertheless, the parties proceed with the transaction. [Comment 1 was amended in 1966.]

2. Under this Article a proposed deal which in commercial understanding has in fact been closed is recognized as a contract. Therefore, any additional matter contained in the confirmation or in the acceptance falls within subsection (2) and must be regarded as a proposal for an added term unless the acceptance is made conditional on the acceptance of the additional or different terms. [Comment 2 was amended in 1966.]

3. Whether or not additional or different terms will become part of the agreement depends upon the provisions of subsection (2). If they are such as materially to alter the original bargain, they will not be included unless expressly agreed to by the other party. If, however, they are terms which would not so change the bargain they will be incorporated unless notice of objection to them has already been given or is given within a reasonable time.

4. Examples of typical clauses which would normally "materially alter" the contract and so result in surprise or hardship incorporated without express awareness by the other party are: a clause negating such standard warranties as that of merchantability or fitness for a particular purpose in circumstances in which either warranty normally attaches; a clause requiring a guaranty of 90% or 100% deliveries in a case such as a contract by cannery, where the usage of the trade allows greater quantity leeways; a clause reserving to the seller the power to cancel upon the buyer's failure to meet any invoice when due; a clause requiring that complaints be made in a time materially shorter than customary or reasonable.

5. Examples of clauses which involve no element of unreasonable surprise and which therefore are to be incorporated in the contract unless notice of objection is seasonably given are: a clause setting forth and perhaps enlarging slightly upon the seller's exemption due to supervening causes beyond his control, similar to those covered by the provision of this Article on merchant's excuse by failure of presupposed conditions or a clause fixing in advance any reasonable formula of proration under such circumstances; a clause fixing a reasonable time for complaints within customary limits, or in the case of a purchase for sub-sale, providing for inspection by the sub-purchaser; a clause providing for interest on overdue invoices or fixing the seller's standard credit terms where they are within the range of trade practice and do not limit any credit bargained for; a clause limiting the right of rejection for defects which

fall within the customary trade tolerances for acceptance "with adjustment" or otherwise limiting remedy in a reasonable manner (see Sections 2-718 and 2-719).

6. If no answer is received within a reasonable time after additional terms are proposed, it is both fair and commercially sound to assume that their inclusion has been assented to. Where clauses on confirming forms sent by both parties conflict each party must be assumed to object to a clause of the other conflicting with one on the confirmation sent by himself. As a result the requirement that there be notice of objection which is found in subsection (2) is satisfied and the conflicting terms do not become a part of the contract. The contract then consists of the terms originally expressly agreed to, terms on which the confirmations agree, and terms supplied by this Act, including subsection (2). The written confirmation is also subject to Section 2-201. Under that section a failure to respond permits enforcement of a prior oral agreement; under this section a failure to respond permits additional terms to become part of the agreement. [Comment 6 was amended in 1966.]

7. In many cases, as where goods are shipped, accepted and paid for before any dispute arises, there is no question whether a contract has been made. In such cases, where the writings of the parties do not establish a contract, it is not necessary to determine which act or document constituted the offer and which the acceptance. See Section 2-204. The only question is what terms are included in the contract, and subsection (3) furnishes the governing rule. [Comment 7 was added in 1966.]

§ 2-208. Course of Performance or Practical Construction.[5]

(1) Where the contract for sale involves repeated occasions for performance by either party with knowledge of the nature of the performance and opportunity for objection to it by the other, any course of performance accepted or acquiesced in without objection shall be relevant to determine the meaning of the agreement.

(2) The express terms of the agreement and any such course of performance, as well as any course of dealing and usage of trade, shall be construed whenever reasonable as consistent with each other; but when such construction is unreasonable, express terms shall control course of performance and course of performance shall control both course of dealing and usage of trade (Section 1-205).

(3) Subject to the provisions of the next section on modification and waiver, such course of performance shall be relevant to show a waiver or modification of any term inconsistent with such course of performance.

5. Section 2-208 has been deleted in those states which have enacted revised Article 1 because it is unnecessary in light of revised § 1-303.

§2-209. Modification, Rescission and Waiver.

(1) An agreement modifying a contract within this Article needs no consideration to be binding.

(2) A signed agreement which excludes modification or rescission except by a signed writing cannot be otherwise modified or rescinded, but except as between merchants such a requirement on a form supplied by the merchant must be separately signed by the other party.

(3) The requirements of the statute of frauds section of this Article (Section 2-201) must be satisfied if the contract as modified is within its provisions.

(4) Although an attempt at modification or rescission does not satisfy the requirements of subsection (2) or (3) it can operate as a waiver.

(5) A party who has made a waiver affecting an executory portion of the contract may retract the waiver by reasonable notification received by the other party that strict performance will be required of any term waived, unless the retraction would be unjust in view of a material change of position in reliance on the waiver.

Official Comment:

1. This section seeks to protect and make effective all necessary and desirable modifications of sales contracts without regard to the technicalities which at present hamper such adjustments.

2. Subsection (1) provides that an agreement modifying a sales contract needs no consideration to be binding. However, modifications made thereunder must meet the test of good faith imposed by this Act. The effective use of bad faith to escape performance on the original contract terms is barred, and the extortion of a "modification" without legitimate commercial reason is ineffective as a violation of the duty of good faith. Nor can a mere technical consideration support a modification made in bad faith.

The test of "good faith" between merchants or as against merchants includes "observance of reasonable commercial standards of fair dealing in the trade" (Section 2-103), and may in some situations require an objectively demonstrable reason for seeking a modification. But such matters as a market shift which makes performance come to involve a loss may provide such a reason even though there is no such unforeseen difficulty as would make out a legal excuse from performance under Sections 2-615 and 2-616.

PART 3. GENERAL OBLIGATION AND CONSTRUCTION OF CONTRACT

§2-301. General Obligations of Parties.

The obligation of the seller is to transfer and deliver and that of the buyer is to accept and pay in accordance with the contract.

§ 2-302. Unconscionable Contract or Clause.

(1) If the court as a matter of law finds the contract or any clause of the contract to have been unconscionable at the time it was made, the court may refuse to enforce the contract, or it may enforce the remainder of the contract without the unconscionable clause, or it may so limit the application of any unconscionable clause as to avoid any unconscionable result.

(2) When it is claimed or appears to the court that the contract or any clause thereof may be unconscionable, the parties shall be afforded a reasonable opportunity to present evidence as to its commercial setting, purpose, and effect to aid the court in making the determination.

Official Comment:

1. This section is intended to make it possible for the courts to police explicitly against the contracts or clauses which they find to be unconscionable. In the past such policing has been accomplished by adverse construction of language, by manipulation of the rules of offer and acceptance, or by determinations that the clause is contrary to public policy or to the dominant purpose of the contract. This section is intended to allow the court to pass directly on the unconscionability of the contract or a particular clause therein and to make a conclusion of law as to its unconscionability. The basic test is whether, in the light of the general commercial background and the commercial needs of the particular trade or case, the clauses involved are so one-sided as to be unconscionable under the circumstances existing at the time of the making of the contract. Subsection (2) makes it clear that it is proper for the court to hear evidence upon these questions. The principle is one of the prevention of oppression and unfair surprise (Cf. *Campbell Soup Co. v. Wentz*, 172 F.2d 80, 3d Cir. 1948) and not of disturbance of allocation of risks because of superior bargaining power. The underlying basis of this section is illustrated by the results in cases such as the following: *Kansas City Wholesale Grocery Co. v. Weber Packing Corporation*, 93 Utah 414, 73 P.2d 1272 (1937), where a clause limiting time for complaints was held inapplicable to latent defects in a shipment of catsup which could be discovered only by microscopic analysis; *Hardy v. General Motors Acceptance Corporation*, 38 Ga.App. 463, 144 S.E. 327 (1928), holding that a disclaimer of warranty clause applied only to express warranties, thus letting in a fair implied warranty; *Andrews Bros. v. Singer & Co.* (1934 CA) 1 K.B. 17, holding that where a car with substantial mileage was delivered instead of a "new" car, a disclaimer of warranties, including those "implied," left unaffected an "express obligation" on the description, even though the Sale of Goods Act called such an implied warranty; *New Prague Flouring Mill Co. v. G. A. Spears*, 194 Iowa 417, 189 N.W. 815 (1922), holding that a clause permitting the seller, upon the buyer's failure to supply shipping instructions, to cancel, ship, or allow delivery date to be indefinitely postponed 30 days at a time by the inaction, does not indefinitely postpone the date of measuring damages for the buyer's breach, to the seller's advantage; and *Kansas Flour Mills Co. v. Dirks*, 100 Kan. 376, 164 P. 273 (1917), where

under a similar clause in a rising market the court permitted the buyer to measure his damages for non-delivery at the end of only one 30 day postponement; *Green v. Arcos, Ltd.* (1931 CA) 47 T.L.R. 336, where a blanket clause prohibiting rejection of shipments by the buyer was restricted to apply to shipments where discrepancies represented merely mercantile variations; *Meyer v. Packard Cleveland Motor Co.*, 106 Ohio St. 328, 140 N.E. 118 (1922), in which the court held that a "waiver" of all agreements not specified did not preclude implied warranty of fitness of a rebuilt dump truck for ordinary use as a dump truck; *Austin Co. v. J. H. Tillman Co.*, 104 Or. 541, 209 P. 131 (1922), where a clause limiting the buyer's remedy to return was held to be applicable only if the seller had delivered a machine needed for a construction job which reasonably met the contract description; *Bekkevold v. Potts*, 173 Minn. 87, 216 N.W. 790, 59 A.L.R. 1164 (1927), refusing to allow warranty of fitness for purpose imposed by law to be negated by clause excluding all warranties "made" by the seller; *Robert A. Munroe & Co. v. Meyer* (1930) 2 K.B. 312, holding that the warranty of description overrides a clause reading "with all faults and defects" where adulterated meat not up to the contract description was delivered.

2. Under this section, the court, in its discretion, may refuse to enforce the contract as a whole if it is permeated by the unconscionability, or it may strike any single clause or group of clauses which are so tainted or which are contrary to the essential purpose of the agreement, or it may simply limit unconscionable clauses so as to avoid unconscionable results.

3. This present section is addressed to the court, and the decision is to be made by it. The commercial evidence referred to in subsection (2) is for the court's consideration, not the jury's. Only the agreement which results from the court's action on these matters is to be submitted to the general triers of the facts.

§ 2-305. Open Price Term.

(1) The parties if they so intend can conclude a contract for sale even though the price is not settled. In such a case the price is a reasonable price at the time for delivery if:

(a) nothing is said as to price; or

(b) the price is left to be agreed by the parties and they fail to agree; or

(c) the price is to be fixed in terms of some agreed market or other standard as set or recorded by a third person or agency and it is not so set or recorded.

(2) A price to be fixed by the seller or by the buyer means a price to be fixed in good faith.

(3) When a price left to be fixed otherwise than by agreement of the parties fails to be fixed through fault of one party, the other may at his option treat the contract as canceled or himself fix a reasonable price.

(4) Where, however, the parties intend not to be bound unless the price be fixed or agreed and it is not fixed or agreed, there is no contract. In such a case

the buyer must return any goods already received or if unable to do so must pay their reasonable value at the time of delivery and the seller must return any portion of the price paid on account.

§ 2-306. Output, Requirements and Exclusive Dealings.

(1) A term which measures the quantity by the output of the seller or the requirements of the buyer means such actual output or requirements as may occur in good faith, except that no quantity unreasonably disproportionate to any stated estimate or in the absence of a stated estimate to any normal or otherwise comparable prior output or requirements may be tendered or demanded.

(2) A lawful agreement by either the seller or the buyer for exclusive dealing in the kind of goods concerned imposes unless otherwise agreed an obligation by the seller to use best efforts to supply the goods and by the buyer to use best efforts to promote their sale.

Purposes:

. . .

2. Under this Article, a contract for output or requirements is not too indefinite since it is held to mean the actual good faith output or requirements of the particular party. Nor does such a contract lack mutuality of obligation since, under this section, the party who will determine quantity is required to operate his plant or conduct his business in good faith and according to commercial standards of fair dealing in the trade so that his output or requirements will approximate a reasonably foreseeable figure. Reasonable elasticity in the requirements is expressly envisaged by this section and good faith variations from prior requirements are permitted even when the variation may be such as to result in discontinuance. A shut-down by a requirements buyer for lack of orders might be permissible when a shut-down merely to curtail losses would not. The essential test is whether the party is acting in good faith. Similarly, a sudden expansion of the plant by which requirements are to be measured would not be included within the scope of the contract as made but normal expansion undertaken in good faith would be within the scope of this section. One of the factors in an expansion situation would be whether the market price had risen greatly in a case in which the requirements contract contained a fixed price. . . .

3. If an estimate of output or requirements is included in the agreement, no quantity unreasonably disproportionate to it may be tendered or demanded. Any minimum or maximum set by the agreement shows a clear limit on the intended elasticity. In similar fashion, the agreed estimate is to be regarded as a center around which the parties intend the variation to occur.

. . .

5. Subsection (2), on exclusive dealing, makes explicit the commercial rule embodied in this Act under which the parties to such contracts are held to have impliedly, even when not expressly, bound themselves to use reasonable diligence as well as good faith in their performance of the contract. Under such contracts the

exclusive agent is required, although no express commitment has been made, to use reasonable effort and due diligence in the expansion of the market or the promotion of the product, as the case may be. The principal is expected under such a contract to refrain from supplying any other dealer or agent within the exclusive territory. An exclusive dealing agreement brings into play all of the good faith aspects of the output and requirement problems of subsection (1). It also raises questions of insecurity and right to adequate assurance under this Article.

§ 2-308. Absence of Specified Place for Delivery.

Unless otherwise agreed:

(a) the place for delivery of goods is the seller's place of business or if none, the seller's residence; but

(b) in a contract for sale of identified goods that to the knowledge of the parties at the time of contracting are in some other place, that place is the place for their delivery[.]

§ 2-309. Absence of Specific Time Provisions[.]

(1) The time for shipment or delivery or any other action under a contract if not provided in this Article or agreed upon shall be a reasonable time.

. . .

§ 2-310. Open Time for Payment or Running of Credit[.]

Unless otherwise agreed:

(a) payment is due at the time and place at which the buyer is to receive the goods even though the place of shipment is the place of delivery;

. . .

PART 3. GENERAL OBLIGATION AND CONSTRUCTION OF CONTRACT

§ 2-313. Express Warranties by Affirmation, Promise, Description, Sample.

(1) Express warranties by the seller are created as follows:

(a) Any affirmation of fact or promise made by the seller to the buyer which relates to the goods and becomes part of the basis of the bargain creates an express warranty that the goods shall conform to the affirmation or promise.

(b) Any description of the goods which is made part of the basis of the bargain creates an express warranty that the goods shall conform to the description.

(c) Any sample or model which is made part of the basis of the bargain creates an express warranty that the whole of the goods shall conform to the sample or model.

(2) It is not necessary to the creation of an express warranty that the seller use formal words such as "warrant" or "guarantee" or that he have a specific intention to make a warranty, but an affirmation merely of the value of the goods or a statement purporting to be merely the seller's opinion or commendation of the goods does not create a warranty.

§ 2-314. Implied Warranty: Merchantability; Usage of Trade.

(1) Unless excluded or modified (Section 2-316), a warranty that the goods shall be merchantable is implied in a contract for their sale if the seller is a merchant with respect to goods of that kind. Under this section the serving for value of food or drink to be consumed either on the premises or elsewhere is a sale.

(2) Goods to be merchantable must be at least such as:

(a) pass without objection in the trade under the contract description;

(b) in the case of fungible goods, are of fair average quality within the description;

(c) are fit for the ordinary purposes for which goods of that description are used;

(d) run, within the variations permitted by the agreement, of even kind, quality and quantity within each unit and among all units involved;

(e) are adequately contained, packaged, and labeled as the agreement may require; and

(f) conform to the promise or affirmations of fact made on the container or label if any.

(3) Unless excluded or modified (Section 2-316) other implied warranties may arise from course of dealing or usage of trade.

§ 2-315. Implied Warranty: Fitness for Particular Purpose.

Where the seller at the time of contracting has reason to know any particular purpose for which the goods are required and that the buyer is relying on the seller's skill or judgment to select or furnish suitable goods, there is unless excluded or modified under the next section an implied warranty that the goods shall be fit for such purpose.

§2-319. F.O.B. and F.A.S. Terms.

(1) Unless otherwise agreed the term F.O.B. (which means "free on board") at a named place, even though used only in connection with the stated price, is a delivery term under which

(a) when the term is F.O.B. the place of shipment, the seller must at that place ship the goods in the manner provided in this Article [] and bear the expense and risk of putting them into the possession of the carrier; or

(b) when the term is F.O.B. the place of destination, the seller must at his own expense and risk transport the goods to that place and there tender delivery of them in the manner provided in this Article [];

(c) when under either (a) or (b) the term is also F.O.B. vessel, car or other vehicle, the seller must in addition at his own expense and risk load the goods on board. If the term is F.O.B. vessel the buyer must name the vessel and in an appropriate case the seller must comply with the provisions of this Article on the form of bill of lading [].

(2) Unless otherwise agreed the term F.A.S. vessel (which means "free alongside") at a named port, even though used only in connection with the stated price, is a delivery term under which the seller must

(a) at his own expense and risk deliver the goods alongside the vessel in the manner usual in that port or on a dock designated and provided by the buyer; and

(b) obtain and tender a receipt for the goods in exchange for which the carrier is under a duty to issue a bill of lading.

§2-328. Sale by Auction.

(1) In a sale by auction if goods are put up in lots each lot is the subject of a separate sale.

(2) A sale by auction is complete when the auctioneer so announces by the fall of the hammer or in other customary manner. Where a bid is made while the hammer is falling in acceptance of a prior bid the auctioneer may in his discretion reopen the bidding or declare the goods sold under the bid on which the hammer was falling.

(3) Such a sale is with reserve unless the goods are in explicit terms put up without reserve. In an auction with reserve the auctioneer may withdraw the goods at any time until he announces completion of the sale. In an auction without reserve, after the auctioneer calls for bids on an article or lot, that article or lot cannot be withdrawn unless no bid is made within a reasonable time. In

either case a bidder may retract his bid until the auctioneer's announcement of completion of the sale, but a bidder's retraction does not revive any previous bid.

(4) If the auctioneer knowingly receives a bid on the seller's behalf or the seller makes or procures such a bid, and notice has not been given that liberty for such bidding is reserved, the buyer may at his option avoid the sale or take the goods at the price of the last good faith bid prior to the completion of the sale. This subsection shall not apply to any bid at a forced sale.

PART 4. TITLE, CREDITORS AND GOOD FAITH PURCHASERS

[NOT EXCERPTED]

PART 5. PERFORMANCE

§ 2-507. Effect of Seller's Tender[.]

(1) Tender of delivery is a condition to the buyer's duty to accept the goods and, unless otherwise agreed, to his duty to pay for them. Tender entitles the seller to acceptance of the goods and to payment according to the contract.

§ 2-508. Cure by Seller of Improper Tender or Delivery; Replacement.

(1) Where any tender or delivery by the seller is rejected because non-conforming and the time for performance has not yet expired, the seller may seasonably notify the buyer of his intention to cure and may then within the contract time make a conforming delivery.

(2) Where the buyer rejects a non-conforming tender which the seller had reasonable grounds to believe would be acceptable with or without money allowance the seller may if he seasonably notifies the buyer have a further reasonable time to substitute a conforming tender.

§ 2-511. Tender of Payment by Buyer[.]

(1) Unless otherwise agreed tender of payment is a condition to the seller's duty to tender and complete any delivery.

PART 6. BREACH, REPUDIATION, AND EXCUSE

§2-601. Buyer's Rights on Improper Delivery.

Subject to the provisions of this Article on breach in installment contracts (Section 2-612) and unless otherwise agreed under the sections on contractual limitations of remedy (Sections 2-718 and 2-719), if the goods or the tender of delivery fail in any respect to conform to the contract, the buyer may:

(a) reject the whole;

(b) accept the whole; or

(c) accept any commercial unit or units and reject the rest.

§2-602. Manner and Effect of Rightful Rejection.

(1) Rejection of goods must be within a reasonable time after their delivery or tender. It is ineffective unless the buyer seasonably notifies the seller.

(2) Subject to the provisions of the two following sections on rejected goods (Sections 2-603 and 2-604),

(a) after rejection any exercise of ownership by the buyer with respect to any commercial unit is wrongful as against the seller; and

(b) if the buyer has before rejection taken physical possession of goods in which he does not have a security interest under the provisions of this Article (subsection (3) of Section 2-711), he is under a duty after rejection to hold them with reasonable care at the seller's disposition for a time sufficient to permit the seller to remove them; but

(c) the buyer has no further obligations with regard to goods rightfully rejected.

(3) The seller's rights with respect to goods wrongfully rejected are governed by the provisions of this Article on Seller's remedies in general (Section 2-703).

§2-605. Waiver of Buyer's Objections by Failure to Particularize.

(1) The buyer's failure to state in connection with rejection a particular defect which is ascertainable by reasonable inspection precludes him from relying on the unstated defect to justify rejection or to establish breach

(a) where the seller could have cured it if stated seasonably; or

(b) between merchants when the seller has after rejection made a request in writing for a full and final written statement of all defects on which the buyer proposes to rely.

(2) Payment against documents made without reservation of rights precludes recovery of the payment for defects apparent in the documents.

§ 2-606. What Constitutes Acceptance of Goods.

(1) Acceptance of goods occurs when the buyer

(a) after a reasonable opportunity to inspect the goods signifies to the seller that the goods are conforming or that he will take or retain them in spite of their non-conformity; or

(b) fails to make an effective rejection (subsection (1) of Section 2-602), but such acceptance does not occur until the buyer has had a reasonable opportunity to inspect them; or

(c) does any act inconsistent with the seller's ownership; but if such act is wrongful as against the seller it is an acceptance only if ratified by him.

(2) Acceptance of a part of any commercial unit is acceptance of that entire unit.

§ 2-607. Effect of Acceptance; Notice of Breach; Burden of Establishing Breach After Acceptance; Notice of Claim or Litigation to Person Answerable Over.

(1) The buyer must pay at the contract rate for any goods accepted.

(2) Acceptance of goods by the buyer precludes rejection of the goods accepted and if made with knowledge of a non-conformity cannot be revoked because of it unless the acceptance was on the reasonable assumption that the non-conformity would be seasonably cured but acceptance does not of itself impair any other remedy provided by this Article for non-conformity.

(3) Where a tender has been accepted

(a) the buyer must within a reasonable time after he discovers or should have discovered any breach notify the seller of breach or be barred from any remedy; and

(b) if the claim is one for infringement or the like (subsection (3) of Section 2-312) and the buyer is sued as a result of such a breach he must so notify the seller within a reasonable time after he receives notice of the litigation or be barred from any remedy over for liability established by the litigation.

(4) The burden is on the buyer to establish any breach with respect to the goods accepted.

(5) Where the buyer is sued for breach of a warranty or other obligation for which his seller is answerable over

(a) he may give his seller written notice of the litigation. If the notice states that the seller may come in and defend and that if the seller does not do so he will be bound in any action against him by his buyer by any determination of fact common to the two litigations, then unless the seller after seasonable receipt of the notice does come in and defend he is so bound.

(b) if the claim is one for infringement or the like (subsection (3) of Section 2-312) the original seller may demand in writing that his buyer turn over to him control of the litigation including settlement or else be barred from any remedy over and if he also agrees to bear all expense and to satisfy any adverse judgment, then unless the buyer after seasonable receipt of the demand does turn over control the buyer is so barred.

(6) The provisions of subsections (3), (4) and (5) apply to any obligation of a buyer to hold the seller harmless against infringement or the like (subsection (3) of Section 2-312).

§ 2-609. Right to Adequate Assurance of Performance.

(1) A contract for sale imposes an obligation on each party that the other's expectation of receiving due performance will not be impaired. When reasonable grounds for insecurity arise with respect to the performance of either party, the other may demand in writing adequate assurance of due performance and until the party receives such assurance may if commercially reasonable suspend any performance for which it has not already received the agreed return.

(2) Between merchants, the reasonableness of grounds for insecurity and the adequacy of any assurance offered shall be determined according to commercial standards.

(3) Acceptance of any improper delivery or payment does not prejudice the aggrieved party's right to demand adequate assurance of future performance.

(4) After receipt of a justified demand, failure to provide within a reasonable time not exceeding 30 days such assurance of due performance as is adequate under the circumstances of the particular case is a repudiation of the contract.

§ 2-610. Anticipatory Repudiation.

When either party repudiates the contract with respect to a performance not yet due the loss of which will substantially impair the value of the contract to the other, the aggrieved party may

(a) for a commercially reasonable time await performance by the repudiating party; or

(b) resort to any remedy for breach (Section 2-703 or Section 2-711), even though he has notified the repudiating party that he would await the latter's performance and has urged retraction; and

(c) in either case suspend his own performance or proceed in accordance with the provisions of this Article on the seller's right to identify goods to the contract notwithstanding breach or to salvage unfinished goods (Section 2-704).

§ 2-611. Retraction of Anticipatory Repudiation.

(1) Until the repudiating party's next performance is due he can retract his repudiation unless the aggrieved party has since the repudiation cancelled or materially changed his position or otherwise indicated that he considers the repudiation final.

(2) Retraction may be by any method which clearly indicates to the aggrieved party that the repudiating party intends to perform, but must include any assurance justifiably demanded under the provisions of this Article (Section 2-609).

(3) Retraction reinstates the repudiating party's rights under the contract with due excuse and allowance to the aggrieved party for any delay occasioned by the repudiation.

§ 2-613. Casualty to Identified Goods.

Where the contract requires for its performance goods identified when the contract is made, and the goods suffer casualty without fault of either party before the risk of loss passes to the buyer, . . . then:

(a) if the loss is total the contract is avoided; and

(b) if the loss is partial or the goods have so deteriorated that they no longer conform to the contract, the buyer may nevertheless demand inspection and at the buyer's option either treat the contract as avoided or accept the goods with due allowance from the contract price for the deterioration or the deficiency in quantity but without further right against the seller.

Purposes of Changes:

1. Where goods whose continued existence is presupposed by the agreement are destroyed without fault of either party, the buyer is relieved from his obligation but may at his option take the surviving goods at a fair adjustment. "Fault" is intended to include negligence and not merely willful wrong. The buyer is expressly given the right to inspect the goods in order to determine whether he wishes to avoid the contract entirely or to take the goods with a price adjustment.

2. The section applies whether the goods were already destroyed at the time of contracting without the knowledge of either party or whether they are destroyed subsequently but before the risk of loss passes to the buyer. Where under the agreement, including of course usage of trade, the risk has passed to the buyer before the casualty, the section has no application. Beyond this, the essential question in determining whether the rules of this section are to be applied is whether the seller has or has not undertaken the responsibility for the continued existence of the goods in proper condition through the time of agreed or expected delivery.

. . .

§ 2-614. Substituted Performance.

(1) If without fault of either party the agreed berthing, loading, or unloading facilities fail or an agreed type of carrier becomes unavailable or the agreed manner of performance otherwise becomes commercially impracticable but a commercially reasonable substitute is available, such substitute performance must be tendered and accepted.

(2) If the agreed means or manner of payment fails because of domestic or foreign governmental regulation, the seller may withhold or stop delivery unless the buyer provides a means or manner of payment which is commercially a substantial equivalent. If delivery has already been taken, payment by the means or in the manner provided by the regulation discharges the buyer's obligation unless the regulation is discriminatory, oppressive, or predatory.

§ 2-615. Excuse by Failure of Presupposed Conditions.

Except to the extent that a seller may have assumed a greater obligation and subject to Section 2-614:

(a) Delay in delivery or non-delivery in whole or in part by a seller who complies with paragraphs (b) and (c) is not a breach of the seller's duty under a contract for sale if performance as agreed has been made impracticable by the occurrence of a contingency the nonoccurrence of which was a basic assumption on which the contract was made or by compliance in good faith with any applicable foreign or domestic governmental regulation or order whether or not it later proves to be invalid.

(b) Where the causes mentioned in paragraph (a) affect only a part of the seller's capacity to perform, he must allocate production and deliveries among his customers but may at his option include regular customers not then under contract as well as its own requirements for further manufacture. He may so allocate in any manner which is fair and reasonable.

(c) The seller must notify the buyer seasonably that there will be delay or nonperformance and, if allocation is required under paragraph (b), of the estimated quota thus made available for the buyer.

PART 7. REMEDIES

§ 2-703. Seller's Remedies in General.

Where the buyer wrongfully rejects or revokes acceptance of goods or fails to make a payment due on or before delivery or repudiates with respect to a part or the whole, then with respect to any goods directly affected and, if the breach is of the whole contract (Section 2-612), then also with respect to the whole undelivered balance, the aggrieved seller may

(a) withhold delivery of such goods;

(b) stop delivery by any bailee as hereafter provided (Section 2-705);

(c) proceed under the next section respecting goods still unidentified to the contract;

(d) resell and recover damages as hereafter provided (Section 2-706);

(e) recover damages for non-acceptance (Section 2-708) or in a proper case the price (Section 2-709);

(f) cancel.

§ 2-706. Seller's Resale Including Contract for Resale.

(1) Under the conditions stated in Section 2-703 on seller's remedies, the seller may resell the goods concerned or the undelivered balance thereof. Where the resale is made in good faith and in a commercially reasonable manner, the seller may recover the difference between the resale price and the contract price together with any incidental damages allowed under the provisions of this Article (Section 2-710), but less expenses saved in consequence of the buyer's breach.

. . .

§ 2-708. Seller's Damages for Non-Acceptance or Repudiation.

(1) Subject to subsection (2) and to the provisions of this Article with respect to proof of market price (Section 2-723), the measure of damages for non-acceptance or repudiation by the buyer is the difference between the market price at the time and place for tender and the unpaid contract price together with any incidental damages provided in this Article (Section 2-710), but less expenses saved in consequence of the buyer's breach; and

(2) If the measure of damages provided in subsection (1) is inadequate to put the seller in as good a position as performance would have done, then the measure of damages is the profit (including reasonable overhead) which the seller would have made from full performance by the buyer, together with any incidental or consequential damages provided in this Article (Section 2-710), due allowance for costs reasonably incurred and due credit for payments or proceeds of resale.

§ 2-709. Action for the Price.

(1) When the buyer fails to pay the price as it becomes due, the seller may recover, together with any incidental damages under the next section, the price:

(a) of goods accepted or of conforming goods lost or damaged within a commercially reasonable time after risk of their loss has passed to the buyer; and

(b) of goods identified to the contract if the seller is unable after reasonable effort to resell them at a reasonable price or the circumstances reasonably indicate that such effort will be unavailing.

(2) Where the seller sues for the price he must hold for the buyer any goods which have been identified to the contract and are still in the seller's control except that if resale becomes possible the seller may resell them at any time prior to the collection of the judgment. The net proceeds of any such resale must be credited to the buyer and payment of the judgment entitles the buyer to any goods not resold.

(3) After the buyer has wrongfully rejected or revoked acceptance of the goods or has failed to make a payment due or has repudiated (Section 2-610), a seller who is held not entitled to the price under this section shall nevertheless be awarded damages for non-acceptance under the preceding section.

§ 2-710. Seller's Incidental Damages.

Incidental damages to an aggrieved seller include any commercially reasonable charges, expenses or commissions incurred in stopping delivery, in the transportation, care, and custody of goods after the buyer's breach, in connection with return or resale of the goods or otherwise resulting from the breach.

§ 2-711. Buyer's Remedies in General[.]

(1) Where the seller fails to make delivery or repudiates or the buyer rightfully rejects or justifiably revokes acceptance then with respect to any goods involved, and with respect to the whole if the breach goes to the whole contract (Section 2-612), the buyer may cancel and whether or not he has done so may in addition to recovering so much of the price as has been paid

(a) "cover" and have damages under the next section as to all the goods affected whether or not they have been identified to the contract; or

(b) recover damages for non-delivery as provided in this Article (Section 2-713).

(2) Where the seller fails to deliver or repudiates the buyer may also

(a) if the goods have been identified recover them as provided in this Article (Section 2-502); or

(b) in a proper case obtain specific performance or replevy the goods as provided in this Article (Section 2-716).

. . .

§ 2-712. "Cover"; Buyer's Procurement of Substitute Goods.

(1) After a breach within the preceding section the buyer may "cover" by making in good faith and without unreasonable delay any reasonable purchase of or contract to purchase goods in substitution for those due from the seller.

(2) A buyer may recover from the seller as damages the difference between the cost of cover and the contract price together with any incidental or consequential damages as hereinafter defined (Section 2-715), but less expenses saved in consequence of the seller's breach.

(3) Failure of the buyer to effect cover within this section does not bar him from any other remedy.

Official Comment:

1. This section provides the buyer with a remedy aimed at enabling him to obtain the goods he needs thus meeting his essential need. This remedy is the buyer's equivalent of the seller's right to resell.

2. The definition of "cover" under subsection (1) envisages a series of contracts or sales, as well as a single contract or sale, goods not identical with those involved but commercially usable as reasonable substitutes under the circumstances, and contracts on credit or delivery terms differing from the contract in breach but reasonable under the circumstances. The test of a proper cover is whether at the time and place of cover the buyer acted in good faith and in a reasonable manner. It is immaterial that hindsight may later prove that the method of cover used was not the cheapest or most effective.

The requirement that the buyer must cover "without unreasonable delay" is not intended to limit the time necessary for him to look around and decide as to how he may best effect cover. The test here is similar to that generally used in this Article as to reasonable time and seasonable action.

. . .

§ 2-713. Buyer's Damages for Non-Delivery or Repudiation.

(1) Subject to the provisions of this Article with respect to proof of market price (Section 2-723), the measure of damages for non-delivery or repudiation by the seller is the difference between the market price at the time when the buyer learned of the breach and the contract price together with any incidental and consequential damages provided in this Article (Section 2-715), but less expenses saved in consequence of the seller's breach.

(2) Market price is to be determined as of the place for tender or, in cases of rejection after arrival or revocation of acceptance, as of the place of arrival.

§ 2-715. Buyer's Incidental and Consequential Damages.

(1) Incidental damages resulting from the seller's breach include expenses reasonably incurred in inspection, receipt, transportation and care and custody of goods rightfully rejected, any commercially reasonable charges, expenses or commissions in connection with effecting cover and any other reasonable expense incident to the delay or other breach.

(2) Consequential damages resulting from the seller's breach include

(a) any loss resulting from general or particular requirements and needs of which the seller at the time of contracting had reason to know and which could not reasonably be prevented by cover or otherwise; and

(b) injury to person or property proximately resulting from any breach of warranty.

§ 2-716. Buyer's Right to Specific Performance or Replevin.

(1) Specific performance may be decreed where the goods are unique or in other proper circumstances.

(2) The decree for specific performance may include such terms and conditions as to payment of the price, damages, or other relief as the court may deem just.

(3) The buyer has a right of replevin for goods identified to the contract if after reasonable effort the buyer is unable to effect cover for such goods or the circumstances reasonably indicate that such effort will be unavailing or if the goods have been shipped under reservation and satisfaction of the security interest in them has been made or tendered. In the case of goods bought for personal, family, or household purposes, the buyer's right of replevin vests upon acquisition of a special property, even if the seller had not then repudiated or failed to deliver.

Official Comment:

1. The present section continues in general prior policy as to specific performance and injunction against breach. However, without intending to impair in any way the exercise of the court's sound discretion in the matter, this Article seeks to further a more liberal attitude than some courts have shown in connection with the specific performance of contracts of sale.

2. In view of this Article's emphasis on the commercial feasibility of replacement, a new concept of what are "unique" goods is introduced under this section. Specific performance is no longer limited to goods which are already specific or ascertained at the time of contracting. The test of uniqueness under this section must be made in terms of the total situation which characterizes the contract. Output and requirements contracts involving a particular or peculiarly available source or market present today the typical commercial specific performance situation, as contrasted with

contracts for the sale of heirlooms or priceless works of art which were usually involved in the older cases. However, uniqueness is not the sole basis of the remedy under this section for the relief may also be granted "in other proper circumstances" and inability to cover is strong evidence of "other proper circumstances".

§ 2-718. Liquidation or Limitation of Damages; Deposits.

(1) Damages for breach by either party may be liquidated in the agreement but only at an amount that is reasonable in the light of the anticipated or actual harm caused by the breach, the difficulties of proof of loss, and the inconvenience or nonfeasibility of otherwise obtaining an adequate remedy. A term fixing unreasonably large liquidated damages is void as a penalty.

(2) Where the seller justifiably withholds delivery of goods because of the buyer's breach, the buyer is entitled to restitution of any amount by which the sum of the buyer's payments exceeds

(a) the amount to which the seller is entitled by virtue of terms liquidating the seller's damages in accordance with subsection (1), or

(b) in the absence of such terms, twenty per cent of the value of the total performance for which the buyer is obliged under the contract or $500, whichever is smaller.

(3) The buyer's right to restitution under subsection (2) is subject to offset to the extent that the seller establishes:

(a) a right to recover damages under the provisions of this Article other than subsection (1); and

(b) the amount or value of any benefits received by the buyer directly or indirectly by reason of the contract.

(4) Where a seller has received payment in goods, their reasonable value or the proceeds of their resale shall be treated as payments for the purposes of subsection (2); but if the seller has notice of the buyer's breach before reselling goods received in part performance, the seller's resale is subject to the conditions in this Article on resale by an aggrieved seller (Section 2-706).

§ 2-719. Contractual Modification or Limitation of Remedy.

(1) Subject to the provisions of subsections (2) and (3) of this section and of the preceding section on liquidation and limitation of damages,

(a) the agreement may provide for remedies in addition to or in substitution for those provided in this Article and may limit or alter the measure of damages recoverable under this Article, as by limiting the buyer's remedies to return of the goods and repayment of the price or to repair and replacement of non-conforming goods or parts; and

(b) resort to a remedy as provided is optional unless the remedy is expressly agreed to be exclusive, in which case it is the sole remedy.

(2) Where circumstances cause an exclusive or limited remedy to fail of its essential purpose, remedy may be had as provided in this Act.

(3) Consequential damages may be limited or excluded unless the limitation or exclusion is unconscionable. Limitation of consequential damages for injury to the person in the case of consumer goods is prima facie unconscionable but limitation of damages where the loss is commercial is not.

§ 2-723. Proof of Market Price; Time and Place.

(1) If an action based on anticipatory repudiation comes to trial before the time for performance with respect to some or all of the goods, any damages based on market price (Section 2-708 or Section 2-713) shall be determined according to the price of such goods prevailing at the time when the aggrieved party learned of the repudiation.

(2) If evidence of a price prevailing at the times or places described in this Article is not readily available, the price prevailing within any reasonable time before or after the time described or at any other place that in commercial judgment or under usage of trade would serve as a reasonable substitute for the one described may be used, making any proper allowance for the cost of transporting the goods to or from the other place.

(3) Evidence of a relevant price prevailing at a time or place other than the one described in this Article offered by one party is not admissible unless and until he has given the other party such notice as the court finds sufficient to prevent unfair surprise.

§ 2-724. Admissibility of Market Quotations.

Whenever the prevailing price or value of any goods regularly bought and sold in any established commodity market is in issue, reports in official publications or trade journals or in newspapers or periodicals of general circulation published as the reports of such market shall be admissible in evidence. The circumstances of the preparation of such a report may be shown to affect its weight but not its admissibility.

§ 2-725. Statute of Limitations in Contracts for Sale.

(1) Except as otherwise provided in this section, an action for breach of any contract for sale must be commenced within four years after the right of action has accrued. By the original agreement the parties may reduce the period of limitation to not less than one year but may not extend it.

. . .